The Man I Didn't Know

by
Dr. Art Schmitt
and
Marie Leduc

To order additional copies, please contact us.
BookSurge, LLC
www.booksurge.com
1-866-308-6235
orders@booksurge.com

A Foreword …

This book should be required reading for all spouses of war veterans. The wives of the Vietnam War indeed have compelling stories to tell and a treasure of wisdom to impart to the next generation of combat wives. So much has been learned about Post Traumatic Stress Disorder and its toxic effect on family life and particularly marital life. In reading these stories you will see a continuous thread binding these women together. We have already seen statistics on how many marriages are being torn apart today when soldiers come home from war. The veteran is not the same person he was when he went to war, and yet, unsuspectingly, the wife expects to see the same man she sent off. Not so. Let me reiterate that I believe this book should be required reading for all combat wives. I use the term "combat wives" to imply that once the joy of the homecoming subsides, a new war may ensue – the war to reconnect, reestablish and rebuild the marriage through loving patience, listening ears, sharpened insights and open dialogue – the ultimate battle to save the marriage. The wives in this book have their own battle scars and war wounds and have loved enough and believed enough to be the glue that held their marriages together. These women deserve the Purple Hearts, the Bronze Stars, and the commendation medals and yet all they really want is their husband's love, friendship and companionship.

Father Philip G. Salois, M.S.
National Chaplain, Vietnam Veterans of America
Founder, National Conference of Vietnam Veteran Ministers

In Recognition

The poems for this book have been written by the artists, my daughter, Melody Grell, my stepdaughter, Julie Smith Koos, my co-author, Marie Leduc, and Pete Frease. They were written independently of the book, *The Man I Didn't Know*, prior to the conception of this manuscript. After reading them it became apparent they were fitting and appropriate to use and they must be included in the book, paying tribute to the wives and families affected by Post Traumatic Stress Disorder and struggling to maintain the status quo. Thank you Melody Grell, Julie Smith Koos, Pete Frease, and Marie Leduc for contributing their artistry to this book.

In addition I would like to thank Laura Ellis for providing the two pictures for the back cover of the Wall and the women soldiers. Wiley Harris should be recognized for the Helo at sunset picture on the front cover. I would be remiss if I didn't recognize Brandi Laughey for the exquisite graphic design on both the front and back cover for my first book and this one. The biggest tribute and thanks should go to the wives and families who contributed their stories to help others who lived this life of PTSD. We also would like to thank Father Philip Salois for writing such a wonderful foreword to the book.

An extra special thanks to Marie Leduc who inspired me to write this book and has been of invaluable assistance as my co-author. Thank you one and all for your magnificent contribution.

Special thanks to Ruth Coleman for her expertise and an exceptional job editing the manuscript. I would also like to thank my wife, Marilyn, who was patient and helpful as we worked on the book.

Art Schmitt

While writing this book, I thought of the many veterans and families I have met, each with their own story, and I shed tears as I read some of the stories wives and families shared for this book. I want to thank all of these people for letting me be a part of their lives.

I would also like to thank Roy Driver and Jim Kelly, the two counselors who helped me understand PTSD and taught me "You are special!"

To Ruth Coleman, my best friend, for keeping me sane through the correcting and proofreading of this book, but also for always being there, whenever I needed her, since we met in our freshman year of high school … a special thank you.

To my sons, Thom and Geoff, for just being the wonderful sons they are. They may not understand how they have helped me get through so many tough times, just because of my love for them.

And so much love and thanks goes to my husband George, for his love and kindness and his support throughout the writing of this book.

Last, to Art Schmitt, who helped me to make a dream come true and accomplish one of my goals in life by him writing and asking me to co-author *The Man I Didn't Know*.

Thank you! Welcome Home!

Marie Leduc

Illustrations by Marie Leduc

Introduction

In November 2003 I had the privilege of attending an Air Crew Honor Roll ceremony on board the USS Yorktown in Charleston, SC. In conjunction with the event I had a book signing for my first book, *A War With No Name*, *Post Traumatic Stress Disorder, A Survivor's Story*. It was essentially about my three tours in Vietnam.

A lady approached me and asked if I was going to write another book. I chuckled and said, "I don't think so, this one took me ten years." She explained that her first husband went to Vietnam before they were married a year. Because of the changes in both of them the relationship ended up in divorce after 17 years.

Her present husband suffers from PTSD and is in treatment. Sometimes the relationship has been difficult. I have now learned about PTSD and have the tools to deal with the disorder and recognize how it affects veterans and their families. I wish other wives and families could understand and comprehend the disastrous results of PTSD.

She asked me if I would write a book about the effects on the family. I didn't sleep a wink all that night. I got up the next morning and started writing Book II, *The Man I Didn't Know*, *The Stories of Wives and Families Who Suffer From PTSD*. This woman, and the inspiration for this book, is Marie Leduc.

Because of her experience and knowledge of the disorder I have asked Marie to co-author this book, *The Man I Didn't Know*.

Dr. Art Schmitt
CDR USN Retired

Author's Note

In some cases, as we wrote the stories, particularly with the responses to the questionnaires, we had to use literary license. In other stories we had to modify the language only to make it more grammatically correct. We tried to report the facts as they were related to us. If we altered some of the facts inadvertently, we apologize.

Most contributors wished to remain anonymous and we respected that wish. Others wanted to use their name, so we acted accordingly. Our objective in writing the book was to show the wives and families that they are not alone and that there is hope for peace in our lives.

Purpose and the Objective of
The Man I Didn't Know

The purpose of this book is to bring home the plight of the un-honored American service-man who served in all wars. In addition, the stories will serve to illustrate the struggle of the unsung heroes, the wives and families of veterans affected by PTSD. The stories show the courage, the stamina, the patience, the skill, the love and sometimes the anger and hate displayed in the relationship. Some veterans survived and some didn't, some families survived and others didn't. The objective of this book is to show how some of the people survived and coped with the ordeal, and to hopefully give you some tools for your survival.

This book is written for all wives and families of veterans of wars past, present and future who now or someday may struggle with Post Traumatic Stress Disorder in their lives.

These are their stories ... showing there is hope for peace in our lives.

The Father Who Wasn't There

The ship would come in. The band would play. He would bring gifts.
   A new toy, a doll, a stuffed animal. Not what I wanted or needed.

He wouldn't be home for long. I never really knew him.

I became lost. Trouble was my middle name. Looked for love in all the wrong places.

Couldn't find my way. No one to guide me.

It's been hard not having a Dad. Regrets are many.

But there is still time to get to know my Dad.

So far I have learned. my Dad is like most parents, you do the best you can
   with what you have.

My Dad is a fighter, not in the war but in life. He doesn't give up.
   He sacrificed a lot to fight for others, so it is only fair that I understand
   and share him with the war that took him away for so long.

He is back now and I am proud of who he is as a person.

Yes it has been painful. It has caused tremendous grief in my life.
   But I wouldn't change a thing because my Dad saved a lot of lives in the war.
   But the best part is, my Dad survived A War With No Name.

Melody Schmitt Grell

A Shadow of a Man

There are times

When I know him

I see the pain in your eyes

There is a presence

In your style

Of a past untouched

The paths that you follow

Are but shadows of a man

No feelings

No thoughts

No body

No soul

Only darkness

Darkness in your step

Heavy penetration

On soft soil

Melting deeper into shadows

That are going nowhere

Walking on shadows

Of a man you don't know

Julie Smith Koos

Blood Trails and Bandages

We laughed at Death, were agents serving Death, for we were warriors. He didn't have to pick and choose: the enemy would sometimes win and sometimes lose; but Death, in either case, would always have his way.

I can recall one evening when the enemy prevailed. Beside a line of trees in ambush lay a single Viet Cong. I watched his hyphen string of graceful green machine gun reach up and bring a passing warplane down a gentle arc to where a mountain-top-spectacular fireworks display of burning fuel and blasting rockets left a pair of pilots' lives extinguished. Death's dark face a grin.

Another night indifferent Death was served again when we pounced on a motor flash and left behind shrubs draped in shredded meat and splintered bone and hair. A morning boat-crew sweep to see what they could find revealed soiled bandage wraps and trails of blood where Charlie dragged away his comrades through the mud. The motor site destroyed, and half a dozen dead, we marveled someone managed to survive this kind of slaughter – never mind the mothers, widows shed a flood of grief, for these were only enemy.

In war there is no glory, Be Or Not Be, in killing, dying facing Death, but only in how well we killed, dying face him head to head.

Pete Frease
2003

Heroes

VETERANS … we all know a vet, someone who served in the National Guard or during peace time, or someone lucky enough to have served during war time in a non-combat zone, or a combat vet, the one who went to war and lived through Hell.

If the vet you know served during WWII (whether in a non-combat zone or a combat zone) he may speak of his tour as just doing what he had to do for his country.

Most WWII combat vets suffer from what they call combat fatigue, but hide their feelings of fear. They may talk about the war and where they were, but they stick to talking about the good times, leaving the combat part out. They have locked it up in their memories for only themselves, the part that really bothers them, torturing them daily. Most vets never learn to heal, instead they said to just let it go, forget it, stuff it away and die with the pain.

Those who served during the Korean War say it is "The Forgotten War," and like WWII vets they live with their pain, never forgetting, yet never healing.

The Vietnam War was fought differently. They did their tour of 1 year (13 months for Marines). This lasted for a period of 10 years, so you have Nam vets living through quite a length of time.

Every day they lived through trauma – death of their friends, or themselves causing death to the enemy, the fear of friendly fire, getting wounded, seeing their friends medivaced out and never knowing what happened to them, fear of becoming prisoners of war, and watching the innocent victims of the war-torn country.

Yes, these are the traumas of every war and the memories are brought home to live with them daily, but Nam vets lived one more trauma. They were sent back to "the world" after one year. One day at war, the next day back home. They were left with the guilt of leaving while the war raged on, leaving their brothers behind to fight and die. People at home did not understand what war was really like, and they expected the vet to adjust immediately … you're home, you're safe, just forget yesterday!

For many years, like the vets of WWII and Korea, they did forget. Stuff everything, don't let your feelings show, suffer and go crazy in your head, but don't talk about it. The vets feel like they are the only ones who are this way because no one talks. Drinking and drugs made the feelings go away, so many (including WWII and Korean vets) tried using them. Yes, the feelings went away, but only while they were drugged or drunk … then the feelings all came back.

What now, many asked?

This is no way to live!

Today many vets are learning about their feelings. They are learning, too, that this dysfunctional disorder passed down for generations must stop. Stuff everything, don't talk about your fears, don't cry … just forget it. This kind of thinking only keeps pain inside.

Vets are learning to talk about their traumas, to cry and let go of their fears. This takes guts! To relive traumas of your life, to deal with the issues of war, over and over, until there is an understanding he or she can live with.

The memories will always be there, but they are learning to heal the pain of trauma. It doesn't matter what it's called – Combat Fatigue, Battle Fatigue, or Post Traumatic Stress Disorder – I call it … *H E L L* !

*H*ealing

*E*motions

*L*earning to

*L*ove

In 1991 Desert Storm brought many feelings back for veterans and their families. Some of the vets in combat were sons and daughters of Nam vets. The U.S. was again at war! Vets again were feeling loneliness and fears. Families again praying loved ones would make it home safely. Now again we are fighting for freedom in Iraq and Afghanistan. Again we are feeling the pains of war.

But America has learned something from the Vietnam vets … flags and ribbons went up everywhere. When Desert Storm ended, the vets were welcomed home. Now again as troops come home, whole towns come out to welcome "their veterans" home.

There are also the loved ones, especially the wives and now husbands too, who never went to war, but go through their own kind of trauma of loneliness and fear, wondering if the next knock on the door could be someone telling them their veteran has been killed (KIA) or is missing (MIA) or has been taken as prisoner (POW).

Their trauma is also real, and they need to talk about their feelings. Anyone who now lives with a veteran who suffers from PTSD needs to learn about the symptoms and to understand them … knowing they are not alone. Millions of veterans have gone to war so there are millions of families who suffer the pains of PTSD.

The following stories and poems are about the heroes and their families. The heroes who fight to keep America free are still fighting today to heal the traumas of war – they are fighting our own government for their rights and benefits, fighting to find answers about our missing in action (MIAs), and for those who never went to war, but have sent their loved ones to fight and then live with the symptoms of PTSD when it is brought back to our homes.

Yes, we all know a veteran, the wives, husbands, mothers and fathers, brothers and sisters, and the children of these veterans … they should all be known as heroes!!!

We should all be saying, "Thank you! Welcome Home!"

Marie Leduc

Historical Perspective

Prior to the Civil War, Post Traumatic Stress Disorder was called railroad hysteria. During the Civil War it was called soldiers heart. World War I PTSD was called shell shock, and during World War II it was called battle fatigue.

The psychologist bible DSM I, first published in 1952, characterized the disorder as stress response syndrome. In 1968 DSM II deleted stress response syndrome and called it adjustment reaction to adult life. Finally in 1980 DSM called it Post Traumatic Stress Disorder. In 1987 DSM III-R through the present gives the definition as PTSD: A traumatic event can lead to and involve threat to one's life. Fear, helplessness or horror. Reexperiencing the event time and time again. Avoidance of things associated with the event. Significant distress and increased arousal, impaired social or occupational functioning, emotional numbing, sleep disturbance with nightmares.

The following concerns *Vietnam Fact vs. Fiction* by Bruce Dyer. A surprisingly high number of men and women who have claimed to serve in Vietnam actually did not serve. The purpose of Mr. Dyer speaking out is to enlighten the people of America to real facts vs. the fictional events in *The War With No Name* by Dr. Art Schmitt (booksurge.com).

The medal of honor was awarded to 240 men. The number killed was 58,148; 75,000 were severely disabled, 23,214 were 100% disabled (and the number grows as we speak), and 5,283 lost limbs. Of those killed, 61% were younger than 21, 11,465 were younger than 20 years old; of those killed 17,539 were married; five men killed in Vietnam were only 16 years old, 1,875 are still unaccounted for, 97% were honorably discharged, and 74% said they would serve again, even knowing the outcome. Vietnam vets have lower unemployment rates than the same non-vet age group; 87% of Americans hold Vietnam vets in high esteem. According to the 1995 census, 1,713,823 of those who served in Vietnam were still alive.

Served in Vietnam, 1995 Census – 1,713,823

Falsely claiming to have served in Vietnam – 9,492,958

Served in the Armed Forces August 1965 - May 1975 – 9,087,000

Served in Vietnam – 2,709,918

Falsely claiming to have served in Vietnam – 2000 Census 13,853,027

It is believed that all Vietnam veterans were drafted; the truth is that 2/3 of them volunteered. It is also believed that 50,000 to 100,000 veterans have committed suicide; the truth of the matter is that the number is closer to 9,000. It is a myth that most of the men killed in the war were black; the truth is that 86% were Caucasian, 12.5% were black, and 1.2% other races. It is also believed that the war was fought largely by the poor and uneducated. The fact is that 78% of the veterans were high school graduates, servicemen from well-to-do areas had a slightly higher risk of getting killed because they were more likely to be pilots or infantry officers. It was a common belief that fighting in Vietnam was not as intense as WWII, as they fought an average of 40 days of combat in four years. In Vietnam we fought 240 days in one year. MEDEVAC helos flew over 500,000 missions. Over 900,000 patients were airlifted. Because of the helicopter, less than 1% died if they were airlifted within 24 hours. Many atrocities were reported by the media when in actuality there were very few. The United States did not lose the war in Vietnam, the South Vietnamese did. The last American troops left Vietnam on March 29, 1973. We did not lose the war … we stopped fighting. We signed a peace settlement in Paris on January 27, 1973 so that our POWs would be released. The war went on until April 1975 when 140,000 Vietnamese were evacuated during the Fall of Saigon. The casualties were almost twice as many (mainly in Cambodia) after the United States left in 1973 as compared to the previous ten years prior to the U.S. leaving. The media misrepresented the war to the American people in almost every incidence. In particular they called TET a major loss for the U.S. Nothing could be further from the truth. The death toll for the NVA during TET was 45,000, which resulted in the complete destruction of the Viet Cong elements in South Vietnam. The only success with regard to the TET offensive was the misrepresentation of TET to the American public. It appears as though the news media is accomplishing the same thing in Iraq.

What is learned in a combat situation is never forgotten. Case in point: when I drive on a particular road in the southeast, as I pass a marsh it turns into a rice paddy right before my eyes. The scene of seeing a rice paddy in Vietnam will never be forgotten. There are two kinds of PTSD … acute, which is treatable, and Chronic, which is manageable. More Vietnam veterans, per capita, suffer from chronic PTSD than from any other war. The reason for this is unknown, but it may be that it was an unpopular war and the veterans were not welcomed home. There are fewer cases of acute PTSD since every soldier knew when he was coming home. During World War II, 17% were afflicted with acute PTSD, but with Vietnam veterans it is only 1%. World War II veterans never knew how many battles they would have to fight and they never knew when they were coming home.

It is just a matter of time before the behaviors are exhibited with people who have PTSD. Retirement seems to be one of the contributing factors to the start of the symptoms. Worry and free time tend to stimulate the beginning of the symptoms. Anger is one symptom that is free floating and can be directed at anyone. Flashbacks are a very common symptom. The intensity of the flashback depends on the length of the trauma and the power associated with the incident. In my case, my flashback is centered around the time I killed my first person. It was a bright sunny day and we were patrolling in our helicopter gunship. There were eight people in a sampan and they were shooting at us. We went in and killed all of them; four of them fell out of the boat into the brackish water, making the lake turn a bright red. I see that scene regularly and it is just as vivid as it was thirty some years ago. The feeling of stress on the anniversary of the incident is another symptom. Impaired social functioning, emotional numbing, sleep disturbances, nightmares, and other sights, sounds, and smells also affect many veterans.

For 30 years I was unable to watch fireworks or hear them. On the 4th of July I would literally hide. In just the last few years I have been able to desensitize myself against flashes and sound. I first started forcing myself to watch fireworks on TV and then gradually I was able to watch them in person, but I still flinch with the loud sounds. This is called the startle response. Additional symptoms include feelings of estrangement and detachment from other people. The veteran may not have the ability to have loving feelings. They may have feelings of inadequacy and hopelessness. Concentration or the will to do anything constructive may be lost, along with their old hobbies and interests. Symptoms may be exaggerated if there is a history of alcohol or drug abuse

Historically, symptoms may appear within three months of the traumatic event. In recent studies it has also been found that symptoms can occur many decades later; in fact, more veterans are experiencing the onset of PTSD in their later years.

For a Nam Vet

NAMES ... of those who died
        Etched on a wall.
NAMES ... of those who fought beside him
        Etched in his mind.
NAMES ... of those who have not returned
        Etched in his heart.
MEMORIES ... of a war
        A long time ago.
EMOTIONS ... of feelings unexplained
        As time goes on.
THOUGHTS ... of brothers coming home
        A time yet to come.

I can welcome him home
    and let him know I care.
I can gently hold his hand
    and stand with him.
I can look into his eyes
    and see his pain.
I can listen to him reminisce
    and try to understand.

But I can never take away
    THE MEMORIES ...
    THE EMOTIONS ...
    THE THOUGHTS ...

Nor can I erase the NAMES,
    ETCHED ON THE WALL
    IN HIS MIND ... OR
    IN HIS HEART.

Marie Leduc

To Answer Your Questions

There were periods of time, stretching into eternities, when I wouldn't permit myself to count on or believe in anything or anybody. The action was so fast and vicious it seemed like I was catapulted into an alien dimension. Time was irrelevant, timing was critical. Everything was slow motion and I alone was a prime mover. I couldn't assume anything. And I didn't. I was good at what I did. Every detail was touched, explored from every angle quickly, intensely. The only slack I was allowed was when I was sure I could pay the price of those details I didn't have under control. I was in touch with everything at all times. I only permitted myself to be a vulnerable part of what was going on around me when that homework was done, the facts and patterns comprehended. And even then I was constantly watching, listening to all my senses. My own guts and my pores were turned inside out like antennae. Somewhere in my mind I was always on full alert, finger on the trigger of my reactions, watching any change of details and I would move first, get on it, and be in control again. I was literally able to see behind me, able to put myself between another man's decision and his act … and stop it. Sometimes him, when I had to. They call it war, and to answer your question son, yes, I have killed somebody. What I was unaware of was how by that process I just described, I was also killing myself.

Ed Ruminski

My Story

Down the Slippery Path to PTSD

The slippery path for me began in April 1965. I was aboard the USS Yorktown heading for West Pac, i.e. Japan, Hong Kong, and Taiwan. My first trip, my first cruise – but an aircraft carrier is not my idea of a cruise (no booze, no gambling, and no shows except the one that we were to get involved in). A few days out of Hong Kong, the 1MC speaker system blared out with the skipper's voice. He said there was a little skirmish going on in Indochina and there was a chance that we might stop by for a few days to take a look. This was my first trip to Hong Kong and I was excited, but instead we arrived off the coast of Vietnam. The skipper said the ship would hang around for a few days but we would never set foot on Vietnamese soil. The next day I landed in DaNang – a strange, eerie, but beautiful country. We could hear shell bursts in the distance. It was then that I realized there was fighting going on very close by. That night the 1MC blared out again, and the skipper said we would be hanging around for awhile. Our question was, how long is awhile? He also informed us that we would not be involved in sorties to support the effort in-country. I wish we had FOX news so we could find out what was really happening. We didn't even have TVs or radios that could pick up any information about what was taking place so far away from home. Two days later we were in the Ready Room preparing to go into Vietnam to do search and rescue for fighters and bombers that were hitting them hard. It was then that I realized we were involved with a war with no name.

We flew, God knows how many sorties in, to cover everyone. I was involved in several hairy rescues into North and South Vietnam. We came back with bullet holes in our SH-3A search-and-rescue helos. We were also carrying 60-caliber machine guns, M-16 rifles, 45-caliber pistols, and M-79 grenade launchers. Armor ... what is that? We did have flak jackets, but that was it. I began to realize things were not real and wondered why I was here. We heard rumors of what was going on. It appeared we were at war. (Little did I know that 58,148 lives and twelve years later it would be over). We hung around for three more months getting shot at and shit on. We finally made it to Hong Kong. I appreciated every minute of the R&R, or as we called it I&I, intoxication and intercourse. Little did I know that I would make 13 more trips to Hong Kong under different circumstances. The cruise lasted nine months, three months longer than expected. On the way back to the States I lay in my bunk in the most forward position under the port catapult of the carrier, and I reflected about the green basketballs coming at us from below.

The realization came that it was 50-caliber machine gun bullets being fired at us. Little did I know that this phenomenon was called flashbacks. I just ignored the stray thoughts and knew that I would never have to go back … wrong.

In November 1965 I was ordered to Naval Air Station in Guam. My job was to fly the helo for search and rescue and to fly the R5D, DC-4 transport. Flying the transport was a great assignment – my job was to fly everyone off the island on R&R. Throughout the two years I made 28 trips to Tokyo, 14 trips to Hong Kong, 10 trips to Taiwan, all of the Micronesian islands, Australia and Bangkok.

Oh! I forgot … we were asked to go to Saigon in 1967 and fly up and down the coast doing logistic stuff, people and things. I learned later in my next tour that this was called ash and trash. One three-week period we flew 144 hours. I lay awake in my hotel and thought back to the USS Yorktown and the nice gambling junket we took into North Vietnam. My flashback of the 50-caliber basketballs was becoming more frequent. We could see the smoke of the artillery off in the distance as we flew our 12-hour days in 125-degree cockpit temperatures. I flew in Bermuda shorts, with a t-shirt, a headband, and a 45 strapped to my waist. We had a little cabin up front by the cockpit where we put VIPs, Admirals, etc. One day I traversed the little cabin to go aft and one of the Admirals asked my crew chief who I was. The crew chief said, "Oh! He is the plane commander." Sometimes we had to wait at an airfield for people or supplies, so we would shut down. I could hear the thunder of the artillery and the sporadic sounds of machine gun fire.

I would lie awake in the hotel and listen to the sounds. One day we heard a B-52 raid a few miles from where we were parked at one of the Northern bases. This was the beginning of my hypervigilance. Since I have started this second book, my PTSD symptoms, especially hypervigilance, have gotten worse.

The trips to Saigon were interesting but tiring. After one stay over there we were lined up on the runway to go back to Guam … a welcome thought. I never thought that Guam could look so good. All I had was the crew … no passengers or cargo on board. We were to fly to the Philippines, three hours away, refuel and go on to the garden spot of the world … GUAM. As we rolled down the runway the number one engine, the one way out to the left, started to sputter and grunt and groan. The engine gauges were not looking good. It looked like we were going to lose it on the take-off roll. I looked at the crew chief, the crew looked at me. I had to make a decision – abort and spend an unknown amount of time in Saigon, or hope I could get it into the air. I had just reached flying speed. I popped the aircraft into the air and said, "Feather number one", and I yanked the gear up. We were airborne and at safe flying speed because we were so light. The crew cheered and gave me a round of applause. We flew to the Philippines on three engines, spent three days there, changed the engine, and partied.

In September 1967 I received orders to Pensacola to instruct in helos. It was a great two years. I got to train Harrison (Jack) H. Schmitt, Astronaut, Apollo 17, next to the last man on the moon. In addition I trained Owen Garriott, SKYLAB II. It was a great experience and Jack invited me to the Cape to see him go to the moon. He also named a crater after us … the Schmitt Crater. The problem is that it is on the backside. During those two years my flashbacks and hypervigilance were there, but not as bad. I just ignored it and thought some of those things happen after a combat experience.

The summer of 1969 the Bureau of Naval Personnel called me and said they had a great assignment for me in Vietnam. They said that an Admiral asked for me specifically to head up a slick detachment of brand new UH-1Ls (no guns) in DaNang. I said, "absolutely not." I had already been selected for commander and had one Air Medal. The detailer said it would be good for my career and that we would leave in November. I told him I would go if I could get gun trained in Fort Rucker or Fort Benning.

He said no and off I went to Saigon for the third tour in-country. When I got off the plane in Saigon, the sounds, the smells, the memories came rushing back into my head. I knew that this was not a good sign. I was flown to Binh Thuy, south of Saigon, home of the famous Seawolves Helicopter Attack (Light) Squadron Three. I was greeted by the commanding officer of the squadron. He asked, "Do you want the good news or the bad news?" I said, "Lay it on me."

He told me that the Admiral had decided not to do the detachment but he had four new slicks waiting for me to fly. I cried like a baby, destined to be entombed at Binh Tuey for the 365 days. The number 365 becomes very significant on the slippery path to PTSD. I resigned myself to a life doomed to the palace guard, getting shot at every day and hardly anything to shoot back with. The CO took R&R and I talked the XO into letting me go to Ben Luc for a week.

A friend of mine taught me how to be a gunship pilot in a week. It takes three months at Fort Rucker or Benning. When I got back to Binh Thuy, as luck would have it, they needed an officer in charge at Nam Cam, Detachment One Sea Float, very near the Hue Minh forest.

It so happened I was the only commander who was gun trained, so off I went down the slippery path. When I took over the detachment I instituted a hard and fast rule. I told my men that they could quit flying up to three weeks before they went home and lay around and drink beer. The rule that I enforced was that they could not fly and say, "That was their last flight." I made them go fly and come back and arbitrarily say, "That was my last flight." Every time they said it before the fact, we would be shot up or have mechanical problems.

Without elaborating on the months that came afterwards, I flew a total of 808 combat missions, and got shot down twice. Fortunately I have no flashbacks or nightmares from either incident of getting shot down and I can barely remember them. One was by a ten year old kid who blew me out of the sky with a claymore mine. The Seals got him and killed him, which is how we knew how young he was. The second time I got shot down we took a 50-caliber machine gun bullet in the gas tank. Thank God it wasn't a tracer or we would have been blown away. The first day I was out on patrol it was a beautiful sunny day, we were flying over a brackish lake, and we flew over a sampan with eight people in it. They opened up with AK-47s and machine gun fire. We rolled in and killed all eight of them … if someone shoots at me, then I kill them. Four of the people, one of them a kid, fell into the lake and it turned red. I didn't think much of it at the time because I was in survival mode and someone was trying to kill me.

This scene is the source of recurring nightmares and flashbacks – another notch on the slippery path to PTSD. Other flashbacks and recurring nightmares that haunt me are the green basketballs coming at me. I drive to Savannah from Charleston regularly and there are two spots along the way where there are marshes, which turn into rice paddies right before my eyes.

There are several other scenes that won't go away. One night in a monsoon with a torrential downpour, while we were in a hover trying to do a medevac, we were under mortar attack and the mud was splashing all over the cockpit and the aircraft. The flight surgeon was on board and we were loading the wounded aboard … probably more than we could take off with. The flight surgeon was doing a tracheotomy and the blood was spurting all over my instruments in the cockpit. The lightning and the rain was horrific. It was luck and superstition instead of skill and cunning that got us out of there in one piece After we had everyone loaded I flew out into the rain into the darkness with things exploding around us. What is wrong with this picture?

We got out OK, landed at base camp and I fell asleep in two seconds as my head hit the pillow with every bone in my body aching. The next day we counted over 100 bullet holes in the aircraft. There is a God. I split the crew into two groups so we could alternate one day no fly and the next fly. We had great coping skills, days we were off we drank and the days we flew we did speed. It was our stress management program which worked for 365 days. On the days that we were on duty, when the phone rang we would be in the air and shooting within two minutes.

After 35 years I still experience hypervigilance when we receive a phone call at home when I am asleep. I jump out of bed and the adrenaline rushes through my body and I'm awake all night. As the time gets closer to the end of the 365 days you get a little scared that you won't make it. Thus the countdown to the closing days in-country, marking them off one by one as the time grows closer. This is explained in my book, *A War With No Name, Post Traumatic Stress Disorder, A Survivor's Story* (booksurge.com-author-schmitt). Everyone had a calendar and marked the days off.

The difference between Vietnam and Iraq is that we knew that we were out of there in 365 days, but the veterans over there have no idea when they are coming home. A similarity that exists between Iraq and Vietnam is not knowing who the enemy is. Another similarity is that we still have war protestors. At least these fighting men and women are getting recognized for their service as compared to us who got spit on and abused.

I arrived home December 1970. My first marriage ended in 1975. Could it be that I had changed? During the years that followed and being a Psychologist (never did it full time but have five licenses), I thought that I could treat myself. I started writing *A War With No Name*, but it took me ten years and was very cathartic. It helped to relive the scenes in the book. Once when we were in New York and a Vietnamese busboy dropped a tray of dishes behind me I jumped him and grabbed him around the neck. They restrained me and fortunately I didn't get arrested.

I tried to deal with the hypervigilance concerning fireworks by watching them on T.V. The bright flashes and the sounds would put the fear of God in me. We went to a baseball game on the Fourth of July – big mistake. I told the people we were with that I had to leave and they laughed, but when they saw my face and the cold sweat, they suggested that we leave. On the Fourth I usually close all of the blinds and try to get a quiet place. Two years ago I went to a friend's house and watched them but had them close the doors. I got through it okay. Last year I was in Myrtle Beach and got caught out during the fireworks display. I could not run, I could not hide, and I just held on and barely made it through the ordeal. I have successfully desensitized myself and am now almost comfortable with watching the fireworks, but certain sounds do set me off again.

I came to the realization just a few weeks ago that flashbacks are not necessarily dreams or nightmares. I just ignored the daily scenes playing through my psyche. Recently I started taking calcium and it seems like the recurring dreams are still there but occur less often. I don't know what the correlation is between the vitamin and the frequency of these recurring dreams, if any.

After finishing book one I believed that I was in reasonably good shape in regard to PTSD. I have started writing this book, at the urging of Marie Ledùc. I have asked her to co-author the book with me because of her invaluable expertise. I told her that I only had PTSD a little. Her comment was "No one has PTSD only a little."

As I work on this book the flashbacks and hypervigilance have increased twofold. As I read the stories of the wives and children affected by PTSD I become very heartsick about never having looked at the other side. I now realize that the arguments I get into with my present wife is because of the unrelenting anger, after years of denial and thinking I had a handle on it ... I enter treatment in the very near future. I have slipped the slippery path.

Art Schmitt

Fighting the War …

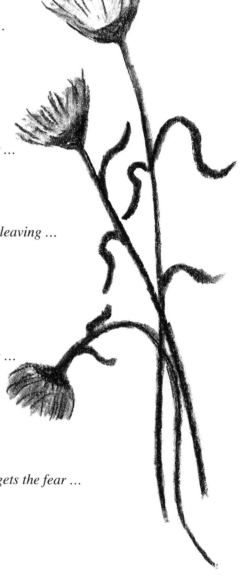

I lived through the Hell of that war …
Vietnam
I wasn't there, I was …
Here in the USA
But, I too lived the days of fear, cause he was there …
Vietnam
Was he safe, dead or alive, I could only wonder …
Here in the USA
Grunt, hooch, kill, Charlie, dinky dau …
Vietnam
Wife, home, love, friends, crazy with fear …
Here in the USA
Time goes by, 40 days and a wake up, short timer …
Vietnam
Counting the days he is gone, 365+, waiting …
Here in the USA
Coming home, back in the world, thoughts never leaving …
Vietnam
Together again, changed people …
Here in the USA
Memories, PTSD, brothers still there …
Vietnam
Nightmares, anger and pain, a wife afraid to love …
Here in the USA
15 years, "Please come home!" numbing out …
Vietnam
Time gone by, years of waiting, divorce …
Here in the USA
Husband and wife, he's still at war, she never forgets the fear …
Vietnam
Someone, please care
Here in the USA
Will we ever stop fighting the war …
Vietnam

Marie Leduc

Let's Come Home Together

I am going to tell you about Vietnam! Now you're thinking, she wasn't there … she didn't experience war … you're right. So, I'm not going to tell about a vet's feelings … I'm going to tell about mine … and how I felt during his time in Vietnam and how I felt when Vietnam was brought back to our home.

Just remember, there is no blaming here, only feelings … my feelings!

When he first came home he talked some about what he did in Nam, and he had taken slides while there. I saw them a couple of times. He asked me to throw out all his letters I had saved. After his return, one of the guys from his unit came to visit, just once, and we never saw him again. Many years later he discussed, with another Nam Vet, the differences of being on the ground as a grunt and being in the air as a door gunner (he was the Army grunt), each saying they would have never wanted to change jobs. In fifteen years that is all I heard about Vietnam. And, although I was living with his Post Traumatic Stress Disorder, I had never heard of PTSD.

Not knowing about PTSD, I just went along with life, thinking that's the way it's supposed to be. We had two sons, and some good times, but this change in him continued to grow.

He was never physically abusive, held a job in the same place for all those years, we had our own home, took vacations, and life went on … So, you say … "What's the problem?" The problem was all of this was from a distance. He had come home from the war physically, but he never came back to me. I think I fought to get him back, but it became my losing battle, until the feelings just disappeared and I finally walked away from the marriage.

The day I walked out of that marriage, I walked into the life of … yes … another Nam vet!

That "in love" stage was so wonderful. A little over a year later we were married. When I got full custody of my two sons and they moved into our new home, I felt my family was complete again. But soon I saw old patterns creeping in, the same numbing out, rage, anger, back to the same old arguments. Two years and I was back to … to what … what was this pattern?

That's when I started to learn about PTSD. My husband went to the Vet Center for counseling. He brought back information to read and we started to learn. It was not easy, because he was feeling the pain of starting to heal. I still did not understand that much about PTSD. I felt alone, like I was the only one going through changes I didn't know much about.

Three and a half years later I was still feeling alone and confused. He was changing, but I was going nowhere. Then, one night in July, at a Prisoner of War – Missing in Action Vigil, I met his counselor from the Vet Center. I asked if he would talk to me … he sat right there on the grass, and we talked for about an hour. He helped me to understand some things I had been questioning, and told me I should read the book, "Vietnam Wives." He loaned me the book a few days later. I cried as I read, and learned I was not alone. There are many women, Nam wives, experiencing the same feelings. I started counseling on August 1, 1990.

My counselor was an excellent teacher. He helped me to learn about codependency, dysfunctional families, teenagers, and mostly about PTSD and its effects, and how to live with a Nam vet. But more importantly, my husband and I were now learning together. We have read many books on all these subjects, listened to tapes, watched videos, but mostly we started to talk to each other and listen to each other. Then, after all this learning, I guess I slipped backwards for a while. It turned out okay; I finally learned what was wrong and soon got back on the right track again. We are still learning every day, and we are doing it together.

My oldest son, Thom, had been away at school for two years. Through his school he was notified of a job and decided to take it … in Antarctica!

In October of 1993 … 25 years, almost to the day, after his Dad had left for Vietnam, Thom left for Antarctica, with an Army duffel bag on his back, for an unknown place where I would have no contact with him except for letters. As he was leaving, the tears started and didn't seem to stop. If I walked into his room, looked at his picture, or just thought of him, tears came to my eyes. I didn't know what was happening … he had already been away from home for two years. Why was all this loneliness, depression and fear churning up now? I really felt happy for him, as we looked at Antarctica as an adventure, just six months, some time spent in New Zealand for pleasure, then he would be back home.

I prayed, "God, please tell me what's wrong!" Then the nightmare came. It was Veteran's Day. I was in Washington, D.C. and I had a dream of my ex-husband – we were at the airport and he was leaving for Vietnam. I woke up shaken and in tears. It wasn't about

Thom the past few weeks … it had been about Vietnam and the issues I had not dealt with for all those years.

Through tears and much pain, I wrote about my year he spent in Vietnam and how it affected me then, and still affects me today. Putting it on paper helped, because a year later both my sons, Thom and Geoff, left for Antarctica. This time I was able to go to the same airport their dad had left from for Vietnam, and say to my sons, "Have a wonderful adventure!" I felt the loneliness and tears come to my eyes as they were leaving, but this time my feelings were different. I saw two young men, my sons, finding their own way in life.

Because of all this, I wrote about my issues with Vietnam. I would like to share this story with you. By sharing it, I hope it helps you to understand the effects war can have on loved ones.

Basic Training

We had been away for a long weekend with friends. Our mail was placed on the stairs as always, but this time the envelope placed on top caused tears to come to my eyes and make my heart pound so loudly, I thought surely you could hear it. I held it close so you could not see it … your draft notice.

While you went to get the rest of our things in the car, I quickly called our friends and told them about the notice. They said they would be right over. When they arrived, you were surprised. I knew why they were there, they knew why they had come, but no one wanted to give you the envelope. Finally, Richard threw it on the table … it got so quiet … for a long time, I held that quiet moment in my pounding heart.

That was the beginning of Post Traumatic Stress Disorder (PTSD) … words I would not hear or understand until years later.

I brought you to the bus early that morning. I watched as you and another friend left for basic training. I didn't know then that one of you would not come home alive.

I had already been to the funerals of 3 Vietnam vets. I remembered how I cried when I learned that my friend, who had lived across the street while we were growing up, had been killed in Vietnam, and two months later two more friends were killed in Vietnam, two weeks apart.

My prayers, as you were driven away to basic training, were "Please, don't take him to Vietnam!"

Each time I saw you during basic training, I saw a different person. I was watching the sweet, gentle boy I had married just 6 months before change into a tough, almost uncaring person, whose words changed from love to kill.

Then you went off to Fort Polk for Advanced Infantry Training (AIT). Those eight weeks seemed endless! September 5th, on my birthday, we were waiting for the call from you to say what time to pick you up at the airport. You called, but it was to say that there was a "mix-up" and you could not get a flight until the next day. Before you hung up, I wanted to know … where next? Germany or Vietnam? "Nam" you said. I handed the phone to one of my friends who had been waiting with me. The endless tears began!

The 30 day leave was spent drinking, partying, and being a drill instructor to all of us. We had one weekend to ourselves, at Cape Cod. We made love, walked the beaches, we were together and I did not want to let you go. I was not ready for the next 13 months of fear and loneliness.

I remember the night before you left for Vietnam! I wanted you alone, all to myself, to make love all night and never let you go. Instead, we went out with the guys, out in the woods as if you were practicing for your time in Nam.

We blocked in a couple who were parking (on your orders) as if we were holding off the enemy. Then you threw cherry bombs at their car. They never heard us until you threw the cherry bombs. You laughed about how we did it so successfully! All I felt was fear for the kids in the car and anger for what we had done. I left and went home.

I don't remember anything after that, until we were at the airport the next day. I'm not sure what time you left or how long we were at the airport … only being there and not wanting to let you go. All too soon you were saying goodbye to our family and friends. Then you held me, kissed me and left…I saw the tears in your eyes as you quickly turned and walked out to the plane.

We all went out on the observation deck to watch your plane leave. I just stood there … all I could do was cry. I wanted you back … one more special look, one more touch … come back and kiss me one more time!

I spent most of my time with our friends. They were the ones who understood my loneliness. They took me out for hamburgers, because it was too hard to constantly eat alone. We sometimes went on picnics, because it was so hard to stay in our home without you. They held me when I cried of loneliness for you. They took care of me for over a week when I had the flu. These friends are still around today. We will always be there for each other. Because of them, I do have some happy memories of that year.

Vietnam

Then there are the memories of loneliness, when I wanted you to be there to hold me. My body ached to make love, to wake up and have you next to me. The loneliness was so bad, I cried myself to sleep at night, wondering where you were, what you were doing … were you even alive at that moment?

You didn't have to worry about me. You knew that I was basically safe in surroundings that were familiar to you. When you thought of me, you could see in your mind, me in the safe environment of our home, our town, with our friends. You knew my habits in these surroundings and when I wrote to you each night, it was of all these familiar things.

When I thought of you, nothing was familiar. It was hard to picture you in a jungle, not our hometown … in a hooch, not our house … with guys I didn't know, not our friends … your habits changing daily to fit the Hell of War.

You knew my daily schedule. I went to mass each morning, then to work, then home… sometimes with friends, sometimes alone. You had no daily schedule for me to follow. By the time I received your letters, you may have moved several times.

I watched the horror of the nightly news, with its familiar body count. It was the only connection I had to you in a strange land.

You fought the enemy … my enemy was time. You counted the days until you came home … I counted the days you were gone.

You listened for the enemy … I heard every noise that creaked, until fear took me over.

You watched anyone who came into the perimeter with caution … I listened to any knock on the door with fear, never knowing if it could be a stranger to say you weren't coming home.

Sleep became restless … perhaps some nights our dreams were the same … of holding each other, making love … only to wake up to empty arms and an aching loneliness that wouldn't let me fall asleep again. I ached to dream that dream over and over, but the pain of loneliness was far greater … I learned to fear the dreams and forced myself to lie awake late into the night until exhaustion would take over and sleep would finally come.

You learned to numb your feelings, to be afraid to care … I also learned to numb my feelings. While you were gone, I went to the funeral of another Nam vet. Billy, the friend you left with the morning of basic training, had been killed.

I watched as Steve, then John, went off to basic training. I felt fear for them as they left, but they escaped the horrors of Nam and were stationed elsewhere. Ruth, my girlfriend who had been living with me, found an apartment of her own, because she thought you would be coming home in a couple of months. Now everyone was gone … I numbed out all other feelings except abandonment, loneliness, fear, and anger.

Rest and Recuperation (R&R)

Seven months had passed and we were going on R&R. I lost my job because of going to Hawaii to meet with you. They said I didn't have enough time at the company to take a week's vacation. They didn't understand the loneliness and how much I wanted to see you again, even if only for a week.

I was there in Hawaii waiting for you. The families of veterans were to meet them at the base. I remember it was very early in the morning; we were all waiting for you guys to come on the bus from the airport.

The bus arrived … guys got off … and then there were five women standing there … tears in our eyes … no one else was getting off the bus … we just stood there looking at each other, wondering what had happened to our loved ones. "Look," one woman exclaimed. You were getting off the bus. It may have been only a few seconds or so after the last guy had gotten off, but it seemed like forever to the five of us standing there. For the other four women it may have been forever, I'll never know … you were the last one off the bus that day! I'll never know what happened to those four guys … and I'll also never forget the tears of the four women I left standing there as I walked away to be with you.

The few days we had together went by so quickly. I remember making love, having you to myself, but not all of you … part of you seemed to be somewhere else, like you were worried about someone, but I didn't understand who and you didn't speak of it, so I just took all of you I could get … it just seemed strange.

We went on long walks, once through a jungle-like part of Hawaii to find a waterfall. You seemed to be at peace there, although cautious. We went to some nice places to eat and we did some shopping, buying souvenirs for everyone, having fun picking out each thing we bought. We also went to one bar fairly often … downstairs, cement walls, loud music, and we always sat close to the wall by the door.

Then it was time for you to leave again … this time I had no one to be with me at the airport … I just stood there alone and watched you leave … R&R was over … you were going back to Vietnam and I was going back to loneliness and fear.

I got on the bus to take me back to the Army base. Another wife who was staying at the same hotel and I walked back to the hotel together. I don't think we talked much, but for the time it took to walk back, we felt very close and hugged each other as we each walked off to our own lonely room … tears in our eyes.

Summer of '69

The summer seemed to last forever. I waited for your letters. You wrote often, but I would get them a bunch at a time, not as often as you wrote. Sometimes it would seem like forever between letters, as I wondered what could have happened to you, but they always came. It was September … I thought you would be coming home soon … and then I received the letter that said you were going to extend for a month and a half, so when you came home you would not have to spend six months at a base here in the States. (If a soldier had less than 6 months left in his service time when he came home, that ended his time and he was discharged.)

I didn't understand how you could not want to come home now. End my loneliness and fears … end the time of waiting to know if you were alive … day by day, minute by minute.

How could you do this? We had talked about it while on R&R … you said you would come home … now another month and a half! I was so angry at you because I wanted you home, safe, with me … I would go anywhere with you in the States … just come home, now! I didn't understand, but you never told me why!

Home at Last

That was 18 months of pure hell and loneliness. I thought the day you came home it would all end … it was only a new beginning of loneliness, fear, and anger caused by the changes in both of us.

I had been warned about this by a friend who had returned from Nam. I remember Bobby saying, "The day before he comes home he will be in a different country, a place he has been for over a year, living a very different life … a life in the Hell of war. His life has been filled with fear, anger, and never knowing what will happen next … but always prepared for the worst. He will leave behind guys who may have saved his life, or he may have saved theirs. He will be so different, you won't know him … give him a chance to adjust … it may take him a long time. Treat him with respect for what he has been through and … love him!"

I heard what Bobby said, but was not prepared for the change. I just wanted you to come home and life to go back to what we had before. His words always stuck in my mind, only I didn't understand them until I learned about PTSD years later.

Because of your extending, I didn't know the exact date you would get home, so I went to work that morning. You took the train home. The station was about a 2 minute walk to where I worked, but you did not come home to me! You hitched a ride to our apartment and called … not me … you called your mother. She came to the apartment to pick you up.

While I was at work, I could feel your presence. I knew you were home! I called your mother, and you told her to say you weren't home!

Why!

You went next door to your mother's to see your sister-in-law!

Why!

Then you even took your mother's car and went to see my mother!

Why!

I was the one who had spent 18 months being home alone … waiting for you … lonely … wondering always if you were coming home … loving you … wanting you in my arms. Where were you? I knew you were home, I could feel you, but I couldn't find you!

I left work and went to our apartment. Our landlady said your mother had come to pick you up. I knew then I had been lied to.

Why!

I finally found you at my mother's. When I got there I just hugged you and cried tears of joy, tears of relief, tears of love! I forgot the anger of you not coming home to me … your response was, "Enough – stop the crying," as you gently pushed me away.

Now my heart ached! Why were you pushing me away?

You had your uniform on, with your medals … I asked what they all meant.

The Purple Heart!

My heart sank. I didn't know you had been wounded! When? Where? How did it happen? Why hadn't I been notified?

You said it happened in June … tears started to fill my eyes. "Don't start crying again, at least I came home," was your reply.

Why didn't I know about the past 18 months of your life? Would I ever know? Would you ever know my feelings about the time you spent in Vietnam?

I finally got to hold you that night, but I could feel that same strange feeling I had felt in Hawaii. I remembered then what Bobby had told me, "He will be so different, you won't know him … give him a chance to adjust. Love him."

I Lived With Those Words in My Mind for Many Years …

How many other stories are there like mine? Stories of "Nam Wives" who stuck out the loneliness of war. We suffered when our friends came home and we went to their funerals. We suffered by not knowing what was going on in the lives of our veteran husbands, while in a strange country … and then he came home and we couldn't understand the changes going on in their lives while here in the States. Because I didn't understand, my feeling was, you're home now, you're safe, what's the problem?

He didn't talk about his numbing out, his fears, his anger, or the war. I also didn't talk about my feelings. Stuff everything!

We had children, but I brought them up mostly alone…as they asked, "Why is daddy always gone – to school, to work, out with the guys, or just by himself?" How could I answer their questions when I didn't know the answers myself?

How many of us "Nam Wives" are divorced because we just couldn't handle the pain anymore? How many of us married another Nam vet, thinking somehow it would be different?

It's Been Years Now … Does it Still Affect Me?

Yes!

I still have trouble being home alone. When I do spend time alone, I still fight sleep. When my husband or children were not at home, I still feared that knock on the door.

I went to "The Wall" in Washington, D.C. on Veteran's Day … I went to touch the names on "The Wall." I didn't see them die, but I went to their funerals and saw the sadness in the faces of their wives, families, girlfriends, and friends. Vets saw the look of death – I saw the faces of pain!

I have nightmares too! Certain dates trigger feelings! While in Washington, D.C. I woke up in tears, shaking with fear. My dream was of him, at the airport, leaving for Vietnam! How do I explain these feelings to my second husband, a Nam vet? So I lay there crying, alone again with my thoughts.

The effect of touching the names, seeing so many vets as they walk with dazed looks, watching them touch a name … I want to reach out and hold each one and say, "Come home, it's time," but what I really think I need is for them to hold me too!

Let's come home together!

The first part of my story, *Let's Come Home Together,* was written in 1993. It helped me to deal with my feelings about the year my first husband spent in Vietnam.

The next part of my story was written 12 years later, about my second husband. I have now learned more about PTSD and the effect it can have on wives and families.

SILENT TEARS

I lay on my pillow

listening to you breathing, as you sleep

My silent tears falling ...

Wake up!

Talk to me ...

Thoughts, feelings, memories

Dreams ...

Need me!

Please ...

It's so quiet, lonely

as my silent tears fall ...

Marie Leduc

Learning About PTSD

My husband is a Navy veteran. When I say Navy most people think he was on a ship. He spent five days on the *USS Saratoga*. That was the only time he was aboard a ship and it was just a few months before he ended his 4-year enlistment.

While in Vietnam, George was a crew chief/door gunner with a helicopter squadron from November 1969 - December 1970. They covered the SEALS and the boats along the rivers of the Delta. They scrambled whenever needed, but flew mostly at night.

Nine detachments made up the Seawolves. George was in Detachment 4 in Ben Luc. He flew around 500 missions throughout the Delta and into Cambodia. At the time he was one of the older guys – he was 22.

He is a combat veteran and saw a lot of action. He received the Distinguished Flying Cross, the Cross of Gallantry with palm, Air Medal with Bronze Star, Air Medal (second – twenty-three awards), the National Defense Service Medal, Vietnam Service Medal, Republic of Vietnam Campaign Medal, Vietnam Service Medal with 3 Bronze Stars, Navy Good Conduct Medal, Presidential Unit Commendation Ribbon, Republic of Vietnam Meritorious Unit Citation, Civil Action Medal, first class color with palm, Army Air Crew Chief Wings, Navy Air Crew Wings, and Navy Combat Air Crew Wings.

In 1980 he exhibited symptoms of Post Traumatic Stress Disorder (PTSD). Today at age 57 he is 100% disabled (permanent total) through the Veterans Administration (VA) because of PTSD.

It has been about 20 years since he first went to the Vet Center for help. It has been a long, tough battle for him … there are battle scars, but no medals for PTSD.

He has continuously sought counseling, went through 2 three-week programs at the VA in Dublin, Georgia. He is on meds so he can stay calm during the day, then at night more meds so he can sleep. He sees a psychiatrist at the VA once every 3 months and a psycho-therapist once a month.

During the first couple of years of being together, I didn't really notice his PTSD, but then again I didn't know what PTSD was. Maybe I was just so used to the symptoms it all seemed natural to me.

But in 1985, George noticed the changes in himself. A friend said he was going to the Vet Center and asked George if he wanted to go along. Soon after that visit he started counseling. He brought home papers and pamphlets for me to read. I was starting to put a name to what was disrupting my life.

Counseling continued for him and I could see the changes, but I still didn't understand enough about PTSD. In August 1990 I also started counseling at the Vet Center, but five months later my counselor moved to Maine. Though I had learned a lot in those five months, I needed to learn more.

About a year later George found another group of vets in Meriden. I again followed him and started counseling there. That lasted for awhile, but I didn't get all I needed from a one-on-one situation. I left there and soon started a woman's group in my home every Tuesday night for three hours. Now I was hearing what other wives had to say. We had a facilitator who is a marriage and family therapist and a Nam vet. We met for a year. Again I learned a lot and what I learned I still use today. Sometimes when I am having a problem, I just think back to something Roy or Jim said and find I can solve the problem. I will be forever thankful to them for helping me learn about PTSD … but mostly making me know "I'm special."

For nine years we learned about PTSD, taught Thom and Geoff, my sons, about it, talked about it, and yes, sometimes we even fought about it, but we continuously tried to understand it.

In 1994 we decided to sell the house in Connecticut. Thom and Geoff were grown and on their own. And even with counseling George was having a lot of problems staying at his job. We packed up what we wanted to keep, sold everything we didn't need, and moved – into a tent. Yes, we lived in a tent from May 1995 to February 1996. We then bought a 5th wheel trailer, which we called home until August of 2002.

During the time between 1995 and 2002, George would go to Vet Centers, Veteran Outreach Centers, and the VA for counseling as we traveled around the country. But even with all his counseling, his PTSD still affects us today.

Let me go through some of the symptoms:

Depression – I think this has been the worst for him. He has feelings of worthlessness, which cause him to have difficulty concentrating, and then the rage starts. He yells at himself for not getting things right the first time and the language isn't always very pleasant to hear. Then I'll hear, "I need a beer." In Nam, the guys usually drank beer to calm themselves after a combat mission. Today, it's usually only 1 or 2 beers, and not often, but it's still a need to drink.

One time his depression got so bad he got his gun out. That time he didn't stop at two beers. This was during the time he was fighting with the VA for his benefits. When I found him he was very drunk. I only got part of my body in the trailer. He squeezed the door so tight, with me in it, and wouldn't let go. Finally, I think because I was crying so much, he opened the door. His foot came up and he kicked at me until I fell out of the trailer. Luckily, we were staying with his parents at the time. I ran into the house and called his brother, who came and sat with him until he was calm and we could put him to bed. My arms and legs were black and blue and I ached for several days. I took the gun and ammunition and hid them in separate places. The next day he was sorry for what had happened. I told him it was the first and last time it would happen with me. He has never done anything like that again.

There were other times he scared me, like the times he drove in a rage because someone pissed him off on the road, or the time he followed someone into a bar because the guy had made fun of him being a Nam vet. The only reason he stopped was because Geoff was with us. He knew that although Geoff was only a young teenager he would have joined the fight to help him, and there was the possibility of him or me getting hurt. He walked out of the bar in a rage, screaming at the guy, but at least he did walk away. He stayed in a bad mood for a few days after that.

His rage got him in trouble at work at times. That was a big reason for selling the house and moving on.

Avoidance of feelings – This was, and still is, the hardest for me to understand. When I sat on the grass at the vigil in 1990 and talked with his counselor, that is mostly what we talked about. The closer I get, the further he pushes me away. This has improved over the years. He has always been so good to me, giving me anything I wanted, always bringing me gifts. If I just said something was pretty, he would go back and get it for me. He is always looking for things I can use. I love being pampered that way. But sometimes I just wanted him, just to know he was there. As I said, this has gotten much better. I have learned I am my own person, so if I feel the "push," I just go and do something I like to do.

Survivor Guilt – His survivor guilt has nothing to do with me, but his moods during anniversary dates can be upsetting. A good friend, the guy he trained to be a gunner, was killed in Nam after he left. For a long time he felt he had not trained him well enough. It wasn't until 1987, when we went to the first Seawolf reunion, that he found out it was a helo malfunction that caused the crash – it wasn't because he hadn't trained his friend right. We did visit his gravesite while in California and that seemed to help him heal from the death of his friend.

Anxiety Reaction – This reaction can be triggered, but is not too often. For a short time, while he was fighting the VA for his benefits, we took jobs together in an investment firm. George did the packaging, but was nearby where I could see him. One day, the kids started popping bubble wrap. To him, it sounded like automatic weapons fire. He came over to me to make sure I was okay. At first I wasn't sure what he was talking about, but I could see that he was very upset. It was almost time to go home, so I told him I was okay and we could leave soon. When we got in the truck, it took me about 45 minutes to calm him down and bring him back to "the world." He quit the next day.

When we traveled, he slept with the gun next to him. I don't think it was loaded, but it was there. "There are a lot of crazy people out there," he said.

So the gun stayed.

He usually keeps a knife on his belt. He says it's in case he needs it to cut something. How often, especially when you are going into town to go shopping, do you need to cut something? I really don't like it hanging there in its case, but I guess it makes him feel safe from all those crazy people, so he continues to wear it.

Sleep disturbance – He has to take medication to fall asleep. Even with his meds, he sleeps fitfully. We cannot have the ringer on the phone next to our bed. While in Nam, when the phone would ring… it meant scramble. In less than 2 minutes, these guys would awaken from a sound sleep, get dressed, and be in flight to combat because some of our soldiers needed help. Now, we just don't have a ringing phone next to our bed.

He dreams often, but cannot remember what the dreams were about most of the time. He just wakes up feeling the anxiety and then can't get back to sleep. When he does remember, it's usually about being trapped and not being able to get away.

Isolation – I don't think George has anyone he considers a close friend, anyone he can really talk to. Well, maybe one, but he lives in Massachusetts and we live in North Carolina.

Most of our friends are veterans. While living in Connecticut we joined with veteran groups who do vigils to make the public aware of the POW-MIA situation. These vets are his brothers, and have become family to me. The vigils take place in the summer, so we see a lot of them then, but the rest of the year we usually spend time alone. If we are in Connecticut during the summer we still try to plan it so that we can attend one of the vigils.

I really miss all of those people, especially the ones called "the vigil groupies." I still keep in touch with my friends from my high school days. Three of them are the ones who kept me sane while my first husband was in Vietnam. I still feel very close to them, even though we are miles apart. Our families still live in Connecticut and Massachusetts, so we try to visit once a year, because we miss all of them too.

This is the one symptom that I think has affected Thom and Geoff. They both chose jobs in far away places. They have both had jobs in Antarctica for five different seasons. Geoff and one of his friends has canoed the Mississippi down to New Orleans, spending three months alone on the river. Together, Thom and Geoff have walked most of the Appalachian Trail, another five months mostly alone.

Thom spent almost two years working a civilian job on the Air Force Base in Qatar. He now lives in Alaska with his future wife, Michelle. He is out in the remote camps for three weeks at a time, then one week at home. As I write this, Geoff and his future wife, Danielle, are in Antarctica, hoping to stay for the winter. If allowed, they will be there 12 months instead of the five months planned.

Yes, a lot of out-of-the-way places, and they both found girls who will be willing to go along with this way of living. They do find friends wherever they go, and have lots of friends back home in Connecticut. I think having a lot of friends is a part of me in their genes, but they still learned to look for those out-of-the-way places.

George and I traveled back and forth across the country a few times, looking for the perfect place. We stayed in Savannah, Georgia the winter of 2001. In April, we were heading to the northwest, Utah, Montana, and the Dakotas, but on the way we stopped in the mountains of North Carolina. We found Hayesville, a small place with its old time town square, friendly people and the mountains all around us.

VA counselors all around the country told George that he should settle down again … find some roots. So here we are in North Carolina where we bought a house. Of course, we can't see another house from ours, and our closest neighbor is a mile away, but I have gotten used to the isolation enough that I also don't want to see the neighbors. It's just peace and quiet all around us.

We have made some friends here, mostly veterans and their wives. George has joined the Veterans of Foreign Wars (VFW), the American Legion, and the Disabled American Veterans (DAV). He goes to the VA two hours away for counseling once a month. I just wish there was a group close by where he could go and talk to his brothers about their everyday life and the things that bother them.

His PTSD will never go away. They don't give magic yellow pills to stay calm or pretty pink ones to sleep to the wives. We have to learn about his PTSD, then we have to learn to cope with him and his PTSD. We have to learn PTSD is not our fault, it all happened far away, but then it was brought back to our homes and many years after a war with no name, we as families are still suffering from the war of PTSD.

I have studied PTSD, learned from reading and counseling…it's his PTSD! I can now walk away when I have to or stay and comfort him if he wants me to. I accept his moods when he wants to be alone for awhile or when he goes for a hike or goes off camping by himself. He will take me along when he wants me there and we still have fun traveling and camping. I now understand his need for peace in his life, so I too can be alone doing crafts, working in my garden or writing about "the man I didn't know."

I am the Forgotten Soldier

I am …

> *the boy who went away to war and never came home*
>
> *your policeman*
>
> *your lawyer*
>
> *your factory worker*
>
> *your alcoholic*
>
> *your little league coach*
>
> *your drug addict*
>
> *your brother who never talked to you*
>
> *in your prisons*
>
> *in your mental hospitals*

I am …

> *the boy who went away to war and never came home*
>
> *your neighbor who has been screaming for 20 years*
>
> *the guy you spat on*
>
> *the baby killer*
>
> *COLD and EMOTIONLESS*
>
> *your son*
>
> *your prisoner of war – 2,400 strong*
>
> *your teacher in school*
>
> *the drifter you saw in town last week*
>
> *your blood donor*
>
> *40 years old going on 19*
>
> *your husband who can't talk to you*
>
> *the stock clerk at your local fast food restaurant*
>
> *your senator*
>
> *your congressman*

I am …

>*the boy who went away to war and never came home*

>*your patriot*

>*your recluse*

>*America's shame*

>*your father*

>*the 36-year-old that died of Agent Orange*

>*DIFFERENT*

>*your suicide*

>*your big brother*

>*your doctor*

>*your scout leader*

>*your ex-husband*

>*the boy you graduated with in the 60s*

I am …

>*the boy who went away to war and never came home*

>*the banker in your community*

>*your building contractor*

>*confused as to why I feel lost*

>*ever alert*

>*ever vigilant*

>*the man who can't rest*

>*the man who fears the night*

>*the boy who went away to war and WANTS to come home*

>*I am the forgotten soldier, I am a Vietnam vet*

Richard Couture

A Long Time Ago ... Today

The Vietnam war – it was a long time ago, but for some who fought, it became a hell they have lived with through the years ... to them the war continues in their daily life.

The first day, as they got off of the plane, they watched that same plane being loaded with combat-tough soldiers, with their thousand-yard stare, tired soldiers going back to "the world" ... and flag-draped boxes being loaded by the hundreds, as the smell of death hung in the air. In unbearable jungle heat, they found their way to what would be their world for the next 365 days ... they were the fng's (f_ _ _ _ _ new guys) ... scared, jet lagged, why-am-I-here guys?

They went to the delta. the highlands, the DMZ, and some stayed out at sea. Some became grunts or tunnel rats. Some flew in choppers and some in jets. Some watched over the rivers, some patrolled the rivers, and medics took part everywhere ... sending those badly wounded to the doctors and nurses, the men and women the wounded never forget.

During their tour many saw, heard, and touched death ... sometimes waiting and waiting. Then one day it happens – Hue, Hamburger Hill, Kontum, Ngok Tavak, Khe Sahn, Ia Drang Valley, Rung Sat ... the whole place goes crazy with sights and sounds ... incoming, tracers, screams of pain and death all around ... somehow, some survive.

For the pilots and gunners, it was a scramble in the middle of the night ... get up ... get going, get the enemy or our guys might not make it. Bring in the manpower, the ammo, the c-rats ... bring out the wounded ... the dead.

River boats patrolled the rivers, checking sampans ... sitting ducks as they drifted up the river. Would there be an ambush? Or would they get back to safety?

At MASH units the wounded seemed to be continuous, hours upon hours of hearing screaming pain or the unanswerable question ... "Will I make it? ... Can you save my arm ... leg? Just let me die!!!"

Special forces all over the country ... trained in warfare to destroy anyone, anyplace. Learning to trust only themselves or their own kind. A oneness in the dangers they encountered.

At the bases or on the ships they watched the guys leave … out on patrol, taking off in planes and choppers … wondering, would they return?

Friends watched friends die, get medevaced out or go back to "The World" … never knowing what happened to them … their thoughts as they sat on a battlefield or in their hooch … "I'll never make another friend … I'll never care about anyone again … It don't mean nothin"!!!

Then they became the short timers ... watching the fng's come in. Some felt they had to help the new guys, remembering what it was like for them ...s o long ago. I'll teach him to survive, were their thoughts … but then, they never know … did he survive?

It's his turn to go back to "The World" with that thousand yard stare. As he gets on the plane, he sees the new guys looking at him. Do I look that different? Do I feel that different? Don't mean nothin. All we talked about the past year somehow seems different now.

Back in "The World" he looks around. People don't know! People just don't understand there is a war going on! Men, women and children are dying everyday! Our soldiers are coming home in flag draped boxes everyday! But to some ... life just goes on.

For some vets life did go on, but for many who went to war, life became a nightmare. Maybe for years they were able to stuff everything, and then one day … just like that day back in Nam…the whole place goes crazy with sights and sounds in their heads. What happens then? Booze, drugs, V.A. wards, divorce, jail, suicide … some can't cope with the pictures, noises, or death going on in their heads.

Some do find help in veterans organizations, Vet Centers, or rap groups. Some find ways to stop the nightmares. Some finally do come home.

But what about those who live with these vets? How do they survive? We read the books about war, about PTSD, about how to heal ourselves. We go to groups, talk about what is happening, write journals, poems, stories. We need to learn how to live too! We need to learn to love ourselves and our vets, so our life can go on too!

If your vet fought in a war, and the war still affects him today, then it also affects you today. Find someone to talk to! Help is out there, you just have to want the help. We have to help ourselves first … learn to love who we are. Then read again the "hell" our vets went through, a long time ago ... today! Remember their hurt and pain, but don't live it for them … just love them.

With hope of peace in our lives.

Marie Leduc

The Final Roll

There were a group of broken things that were damaged long ago.

And no one to listen, so they had no way to know.

These damaged things were cast aside, this tortured group of boys,

And cast into a dark closet like so many broken toys.

The damage lay there unrepaired ... after all they were but a few.

The people's only interest was the shiny and the new.

When someone suggested fixing them, the people all would say

They're not worth the money to repair, that's why they're cast away.

Still there was the small impassioned few that tried to understand,

And tried to help these damaged boys as they aged to broken men.

They were the wives and mates and lovers trying to do all they can.

They are Fog's Lisa and Lou's Wanda and Redcowboy's wife Diane,

And many others I don't know that are spread across the land.

There's George's wife, Marie, who stays with him through it all.

And like all the others out there, helps us rise each time we fall.

They've been stubborn and persistent as each crisis came and went,

Although it has been tough on them, their compassion is far from spent.

So when the final roll is called and set for all to see,

These ladies will be standing tall ... they're all heroes to me.

Terry Lane

On the Wall

Roy called yesterday …

I expected to hear

that smile in his voice,

But, when he spoke

I heard the pain,

His friend …

A brother …

Another name,

on the "Wall!"

Marie Leduc

Tragic Stories

During the 1968 TET offensive, this Army sergeant served as a sniper at a firebase close to the DMZ. At times he would spend from two to five days just waiting in a tree for a target. After he returned home to his farm in rural Virginia he started experiencing flashbacks. He was on medication while he was under treatment at the Veterans Administration and participating in group therapy. Besides the flashbacks he was experiencing poor sleep patterns and nightmares. He had a serious alcohol problem and the VA was trying to make headway with that, but not having much success with him.

After the service he had difficulty maintaining steady employment and only managed to do odd jobs. Now at the age of 40 he resided with his wife in a country home on several acres. His children were grown and gone. He was not abusive to his wife but he was very standoffish and did not communicate with her very well.

He used to go sit in a tree for days at a time with his rifle and a bottle of whiskey and just stare out in space. His wife would try and coax him to come down to eat or sleep, but to no avail; he remained there for long periods of time. One night he came down from the tree and went into the basement. His wife was sitting on a chair upstairs in the kitchen. The veteran shot from the basement. He began shooting bullets around her chair. She sat in the chair motionless, started to pray, and watched holes encircle her chair. Then she heard a final shot. She ran down into the basement and saw her husband on the floor. The nightmare of A War With No Name had ended for him. Needless to say, after the funeral his wife entered therapy for the aftermath of her husband's PTSD. The families are partners in this disorder, resulting in tragic stories like this over and over again.

Anonymous

Reflections on an October Day

The gun truck was a tough old road, at least that's what they say.

But I guess we didn't know that then, we just did it every day.

And even if you didn't want to, you did it anyway.

The fellas that you rode with, they were brothers and much more.

Because you shared what came your way in this forsaken war.

You lived each day together, and you watched each other's back.

Without a doubt you trusted and found security in that.

Then one day it happens, the thing that you fear most,

and there before your helpless eyes, your brothers are all lost.

It happens in a moment, that's the way it seems to be,

it's terrible and tragic, at least that's the way it was for me.

Each time I think about it, my heart just breaks in two.

But I'll tell what I remember, that's as good as I can do.

All thoughts and all the memories are whirling in my brain,

but I hope that in telling I can lose some of this pain.

It started with a food fight in the mess hall on that day.

And we laughed and joked and tussled as we went off on our way.

We played and teased each other on the way to the motor pool.

And we just enjoyed our morning the way young boys will do.

As we walked along together there, we didn't have a clue,

That the hand of death would touch us all before the day was through.

We lined up for convoy that headed for Ben Het,

But they held us up there by Dak To because the roads weren't open yet.

We pulled into a compound so some trucks could drop and hook,

And a couple of us walked while the others went to look.

So we looked for some excitement till the convoy got the word.

Somebody came and told us we could have a chopper ride,

But there was only room for 4 and that we should decide.

Because you see there were 5 of us, not all of us could go,

It sure sounded like a lot of fun, of course we didn't know.

Gary Best said he'd like to go and Neeley and Gamble too,

so Trogy turned and said to me "That just leaves me and you."

He said, "Why don't you go ahead, we can't leave the truck alone."

But I said "No, you go ahead, you'll soon be going home,

And you may never get a chance to take another chopper ride."

And so that's why he went along and that's also why he died.

They all walked out and loaded on, so sure to have some fun,

And then the chopper took off as if it were shot out of a gun.

I stood around there waiting when I heard somebody say,

"That cowboy chopper pilot's gonna hurt himself someday."

"He's coming in here way too hot, he's flying like a clown,"

And when I turned to check it out, the bird was coming down.

The chopper crashed and burst to flames, right before my eyes,

And I will carry that with me until the day I die.

We tried whatever we could do, the fire was way too hot,

With rounds and rockets cooking off, we all might have been shot.

When they finally got the fire out, there was nothing we could do,

that sad day in October when I lost the Minny Crew.

Of all of us that went that day, I'm the only one that's left,

Trogy, Gamble, Neeley and my young friend Gary Best.

I tried to put the pain away, that memory to hide,

but that never really worked because the grief was still inside.

I went for more than 30 years trying to forget that day,

but it's haunted me just like a ghost, it wouldn't go away.

Then a couple weeks ago, I got my memory back,

And the pain is breaking me in two, like I've been put on the rack.

Now I've told what I remember, and that's all that I can do,

So I hope you all can understand what I've been going through.

'Cause when it comes to dealing with pain we've all been through,

I'm sure you will understand ... I know you've lost friends too.

BMWFOG
Terry Lane

Never-Ending Spiral

This story is from the fourth wife of a Vietnam veteran. He was in the Army Airborne and served in-country during TET. He served nine months all over Vietnam, as well as Cambodia serving in field operations and as a sniper. He was offered officer status early on but declined because he didn't want to be responsible for sending young soldiers into battle.

He was awarded a Bronze Star, Silver Star, and a Purple Heart. He was wounded but not hospitalized. Instead he sewed up a knife wound himself and his sergeant dug the shrapnel from his leg, and other pieces of shrapnel went through his arm and through his head. He received the Purple Heart for one of the shrapnel wounds, which was observed by his sergeant, who put him in for the medal. He was asked to submit the other wounds for a Purple Heart. He told them to f – – – off. He and one other man were the only survivors from his unit. They wanted to send him back when he had only 12 weeks left in-country, but he told them he couldn't do it so they sent him home to be admitted to the VA hospital. His stay there was extremely stressful and to this day he is very fearful of psychiatrists, saying he would kill himself before he would go back.

His present wife thinks that he exhibited PTSD in-country, but his symptoms became much worse after discharge. His first wife left him after three years because she feared for her life, and his next two wives left not understanding the PTSD problem. His fourth wife has been reading about PTSD and has some understanding. The veteran was not diagnosed with Post Traumatic Stress Disorder until 32 years after his service.

He will not recognize the symptoms, the major one being rage and anger. The veteran entered treatment in 2000 after a very bad episode, but in 2004 they terminated his treatment because he was the only PTSD patient that the doctor had. All they did was increase his medication.

The problem has had extremely devastating results regarding his family. As his wife so aptly put it, "He didn't come with a warning label, nor does he come with a flashing red light to warn against the decomposition. He does listen and we do have conversations concerning the problems, but he is very cautious about anything changing and fears any government involvement."

Living with someone who has this trauma and the symptoms is extremely exhausting. I never know when his mood will change. I have to watch my reaction, behavior, and moods, which is difficult, because things can change in a matter of seconds. He is very reclusive and stays alone most of the day. Then he complains that I bother him too much. We have a multitude of legal problems, which has been a drain on our financial situation.

The paradox that exists is that on one hand my husband is sensitive, generous, loving and thoughtful, but on the other hand the moment can change and the Dr. Jekyll comes out. On a moment's notice he can exhibit rage, anger, hostility and become unreasonable. These episodes are not very frequent but can be very upsetting and keep me unstable. PTSD is an emotional black hole, which is all-consuming at times. It is a never-ending spiral of good days, bad days, and worse days. Because I have studied the disorder and I understand it more than ever, it makes it easier to tolerate the consequences. My only wish and hope is that an answer can be found so we can bring these men back from Vietnam.

Anonymous

With Shaking Hands

With shaking hands and unsteady step,

I reach to touch the Wall of black.

As though the darkness long I crept,

My body full of life, but something yet I lack.

I reach out a trembling hand,

I reach to touch the Wall of black.

Proudly through the fear I stand,

And then yes, oh yes, I feel them touching back.

My hands no longer tremble, my step is strong,

I have touched the Wall of black.

I had waited and waited much too long,

Now I hear 58,000 say, "Welcome back brother!" "Welcome back!"

Terry Sanders

At His Side

This veteran was married while he served in-country in 1969. He was stationed in I Corp and was assigned to building American and Vietnamese bases. He received the standard citations and was awarded a Purple Heart for wounds received. He celebrated his 21st birthday in Vietnam. He has exhibited various symptoms of PTSD including rage, anger, hypervigilance, short-term memory problems, depression, inability to function socially, occupational instability, nightmares, flashbacks, sleep disturbances, mood swings, and various other associated symptoms. He is presently in treatment with psychotherapy and medication. His symptoms are affecting his entire family. The family walks on eggshells so as not to upset him, which is nervewracking to the family. They will nevertheless stand at his side no matter what.

Pauline Sanders

If You Haven't Been There ...

If you haven't been there ...

shut your mouth!

That's his favorite line.

Well, I have been there!

At night,

when he screams ...

"They're coming through the wire."

When he looks me in the eye and says ...

"Jim's been hit ...

We gotta go get him!"

When I wake up in the middle of the night ...

to find myself cradled in his arms,

he's rocking me,

and sobbing,

repeating some guy's name ...

and

picking another guy's flesh off my face.

I was only 12 when he was there,

But I too have been there ...

over

and

over

for the past 16 years!

Adele Lavigne

Learning to Live and Love Again

My veteran was 23 years old when he spent his year in Saigon, Plieku and Bien-Hoa. He was a crew chief assigned to Mac-V. He abused alcohol and he withdrew from society and lived in the woods upon his return to home. Apparently he was exhibiting PTSD symptoms while in-country and they increased upon his return home. The symptoms were not recognized by the VA for many years.

We met in 1977 and have been together for 26 years. Over the years he has exhibited many symptoms of PTSD, including flashbacks, nightmares, anxiety/depression and night sweats, agoraphobia, inability to and fear of sleeping, severe startle response, fear of death and injuries for himself or the family. He had difficulty with authority, problems with the law, suspiciousness of others. When things got rough early in our marriage, he would disappear for days or weeks at a time.

He was treated in an inpatient VA program in 1989 for ten months. He was hospitalized dozens of times after the program. He is currently being seen by a psychotherapist three to four times a month. Presently he takes medication for pain, to help him sleep, and to calm his nervous system.

In the beginning of our marriage, the effects on the family were numerous. Because of the PTSD he was mistrusting of everyone and was unable to work, which has caused financial problems. He has become isolated from family and society.

The family is not in treatment at this time, but the children were in and out of treatment over the years when things got rough. When the family was in therapy and learned about PTSD, the trust level began to rise. I attended a wives group and he and I attended couples therapy at times. Therapy was very helpful in opening up communication and in educating the family about PTSD. All of these interventions have helped to increase the bonds between the family members.

My vet and I have spent many years helping other veterans to get disability, taking them for medical treatment and helping them with their home repairs. We have had a few veterans live with us and others have come for holiday meals. By helping other veterans he has helped himself.

He has strived to overcome his PTSD symptoms. I think that he has come so far because he has tried so hard. It appears that many veterans just give up. We have known several veterans in the past 16 years who have self-medicated with illegal drugs and/or alcohol and many have committed suicide.

My vet, however, has tried to deal with his PTSD. Although the symptoms remain, he has become an active, supportive member of our family. In helping others and trying to deal with the horrors of Vietnam through therapy, he has found a way to live and love again.

Adele Lavigne

When a veteran sees a map of Vietnam, he can easily pick out the places he has been. These are some of the places wives have been …

VIETNAM

Adele Lavigne

Power of Forgiveness

My husband was in-country from July 1969 until July 1970, stationed in Pleiku and assigned to several transportation battalions. His MOS was heavy vehicle driver – supplying convoys. Later he volunteered to be a driver and a gunner for gun trucks for convoys and engineering security.

The veteran entered the military when he was 17 and intended to make it a career. He was sent to Korea and Germany and was later assigned to Vietnam duty. After Vietnam he decided to get out of the service at age 24. He displayed symptoms of PTSD after returning home but was not diagnosed until 1993. His symptoms include intrusive thoughts of his war experience, recurrent dreams and nightmares, and night terrors of battles that he fought in. Sleep disturbances are recurring and frequent, along with diminished interest in significant social activities, a feeling of detachment, memory impairment and trouble concentrating. Hypervigilance is a significant problem, along with anger and rage responses. Along with employment and family struggles he has judgment issues and poor insight into situations. His therapist has prescribed several different medications to help him with the problems encountered with PTSD.

I met my husband after his return from Vietnam and we have been married for 32 years. There have been financial struggles throughout the years as a result of his sporadic employment, and it is very difficult living with someone who displays a feeling of detachment. Little adversities in life cause overreactions and rage episodes. I sometimes have the feeling that he doesn't care about his family. The children do not understand and take it personally, feeling unloved and unwanted. Over the years there have been drug and alcohol abuse, domestic violence, infidelities, destruction of property, trouble with the law in regard to drugs and assault, extended periods of unemployment, suicide attempts and very deep dark depressions.

Included in the mix of PTSD problems there were problems related to children. The family adopted three grandchildren from a daughter who got pregnant during a previous marriage. These children came from a drug-addicted mother who put them in sexually and physically abusive situations. The family exhibited this behavior because they lived in the house with a veteran diagnosed with PTSD. In this particular family the children were adopted and abused by their parents. In addition these children had organic brain disorders because they were drug babies. The bigger problem in this family was the feeling of estrangement and detachment from the father. Dad/grandfather doesn't love us and he doesn't want us around. This particular man has very poor impulse management and anger control. The children grew up in an environment where they believed they were an imposition, constantly criticized, belittled, and physically abused without explanation or apology. It is difficult to garner up any self-esteem, self-confidence or a feeling of self-worth. These behaviors lead the children on a path of self-destruction.

Through the process I lost my self-confidence and self-esteem … in fact I contributed to the problem. There was a period of self-medication with drugs and alcohol, which led to physical abuse. In addition I dealt with infidelities, devastating rages and poverty from unemployment and wasting of resources. I attempted to leave on several occasions but always returned because of fear. I believed that he was an evil man and would eventually do harm to me. During this period there were several suicide attempts, most thwarted by me.

From this emerged a man depressed and incompetent, who eventually gave up drugs and alcohol. Even giving up drugs and alcohol, he found no joy in living. My husband became extremely dependent on me, almost to a suffocating degree. The guilt grew in me … I felt that his dependence, physical and mental condition was my fault. I started to leave again but felt that he might be successful with suicide and it would be my fault. The financial situation was terrible since we lived on my salary alone.

In 1993, I became desperate and contacted a VA representative; they assigned me a psychologist for him to begin treatment. He was finally diagnosed with PTSD after all those horrible years. The psychologist pointed me in the right direction and I became educated in this disorder. With a little knowledge I began to feel better. It took a long time to separate my personal hurt, desperation, and resentment from my husband's behavior. Even though the treatment program was ongoing we still had periods of struggle. He would take one step forward and two backwards. He continued to have devastating rages and deep depressions but I was now able to detach myself from the involvement. He was sporadic in his treatment and his denial persisted. His flashbacks of fiery plane crashes stirred conditioned response and he would go back to square one.

Thanks to the internet and Marie Leduc's newsletter I have met other veterans and wives and have been able to share and understand the problem with much more insight. His treatment is gaining momentum and he is getting better. He has been able to bring back a suppressed memory of a helicopter crash and deal with the devastating event. He continues to make progress and I do not always understand but I have been able to separate myself from his behavior and not take it personally. I have taken the position that I am part of the solution and not part of the problem. I support and accompany him to his sessions but do not participate…that is not my place. I still have periods of anger and resentment but I can support him with a compassionate, unbiased approach.

I have shared my story because I wanted other wives and families to understand the burden that the families share and the heavy burden that her husband has been carrying over the years. It is important that our society learn from the mistakes of their behavior in regard to their treatment of the Vietnam veterans. It is important that families suffering with the effects of PTSD understand and realize that it is indeed a malady and not a choice of bad behavior. It is also important that people learn the medical power of forgiveness.

This is truly a story of patience, diligence, forgiveness, and love beyond the call of duty.

Lisa Lane

My Vietnam Wife

It's twenty years gone
your going out on your own …
after spending most of your life
as a Vietnam wife.

We've had our good times and bad
Some happy, some sad …
You've been through all of the strife
Of being a Vietnam wife.

Though it was I who went away
to fight that lousy war …
you sure pulled your own tour
you spent most of your life
as a Vietnam wife.

And now as you plan to go away
I wish I could find …
the words to make you stay …
and as time goes by, day to day
I hope someday you can say
that you have no regret
that you once loved your Vietnam vet
or that you spent most of your life
as my Vietnam wife.

Now I know that for the rest of my life
I'll remember the love …
and understanding you gave
and I'll be glad that you spent
most of your life
as my Vietnam wife …

Steve Carney

Finding a Balance

My husband served for three years in the Army, one year was in Vietnam. He was attached to the 101st Airborne, Screaming Eagles.

We have been married for 35 years. We married soon after his return from Vietnam. It has been a difficult life, and anyone who has not experienced the war would not be able to imagine or foretell the future of these men who served in Vietnam. We have a beautiful daughter, son-in-law, and a beautiful grandchild. Our daughter has been shaped by being her dad's child. With guidance, education and deep understanding she turned it all into a positive approach to life for herself. That I am very grateful for and appreciate the outcome.

My vet has had emotional and physical problems that have kept him from working. He is in treatment at our outpatient VA clinic. I worked for over 30 years for the same company, but when it closed, I took early retirement at age 55. The retirement income is not enough so it has been difficult finding another job. It has been a struggle to keep my spirits up while trying to hold it all together, as much for myself as for him. I can't give up, I have worked all of my life for us to keep everything in perspective. To give up would be to die, and that's not an option. I do try to find peace and joy everyday in the small wonders of life and in the quiet of nature. I stay in touch with special friends and family and appreciate the many blessings of life.

I think the best thing I can do for myself is to have a life of my own outside of our home, with job, friends, activities and personal interests. I learned a long time ago that I could not depend on my husband to share much of himself with me in these areas, so to have a life I would have to take care of myself in these ways. Still, it is a struggle at times to find a balance.

Anonymous

My Country

She sends her notes of passion, oh yes her heart is true,

To heal her generation, her love she never withdrew.

Before it is tomorrow, a wide-eyed girl she waits,

In thoughts of love and tenderness,

The day he's home she anticipates.

Friends and family see her, as they enjoy everyday,

Why are they not like her, in school, and work and play?

When it is tomorrow, and the sun has arrived,

The boy that left is now a man, she can see it in his eyes.

This man is tired and weary, his thoughts at times not there,

She tries so hard to heal him, to protect him from his fears.

The beauty of her laughter and such a radiant smile,

Like a flower in the springtime, with the loyalty of a child.

Your days of youth were numbered, no one could for tell,

That the war would grow longer, every day a step closer to hell.

His battles are unspoken as his war rages on,

This woman serves her country, but never went to Vietnam.

And yet she knows the places, names and dates he knew,

But will her country reward her, she deserves her ribbons too.

For when you think about me, and the war I went through,

Remember she's my country, she's my red, white and blue.

This woman is so special, a saint through all the strife,

She's the anchor of a nation, she's a Vietnam veterans wife.

George E. La Bounty

My Hero

I met him when I was 21. He was 32. He seemed different from other men. He was very quiet and never smiled. He worked all day and drank all night. I had just come out of a violent marriage and he did everything he could to make me feel safe. He was my hero. I didn't understand it then, but, he needed to be needed.

One summer day while we were talking, I noticed a tattoo on his arm. Immediately I knew he was in the Air Force. I was impressed! He was shocked at my reaction. I wanted to know everything; When he was in, where he was stationed, was he a pilot? He got a strange look on his face and said, "I was in Vietnam." To his surprise, I was even more impressed. WOW! A real hero! I didn't know any details about Vietnam, only that it was a war. I was only 12 when he was there. I remember watching John F. Kennedy and Martin Luther King's assassinations on T.V. in school, but we never watched anything about Vietnam. My sister married a guy that was in the Army and my brother joined the Navy, but I never heard words like war or Vietnam back then. I remember hearing people talk about the draft, but it didn't make any sense to me. I was raised to believe that it was an honor and privilege to serve our country. From that day on, he wouldn't talk about the war much. He said it was a terrible time in his life and he just wanted to forget.

Well, I married my hero and we have four sons and how I wish I could say we lived happily ever after, But I can't. We had some really tough times. Even though he had stopped drinking, he would lose jobs and we would have no money. He would take off for days with no phone calls and no explanations. There would be months when he couldn't get as much as two hours of sleep each night. I would sit up with him because I was afraid to sleep. He was so gentle, yet, he was afraid of himself and that scared me. He still wouldn't talk much about the war, so I went to the book store. I read everything I could find written by Vietnam veterans. I had to learn about the war from other men like him. I needed to be prepared for anything he might have said.

I began to understand; his moods, his anger and his silence. The more I read, the more I loved him and the more I wanted to take away his pain,

He began to withdraw. The harder I tried to reach him, the further inside himself he would go. Anger seemed to permeate from his pores and surround him like a cloud. He never hit us, he never even raised his voice. He was just angry ALL THE TIME and silent. The silence was heartbreaking. He built invisible walls around himself shutting us out until the silence overtook him.

It took ten months in the V.A. Hospital and us being separated to break through those walls. He still has nightmares and many sleepless nights. He still jumps at every noise and can't stand to be in crowded places. Flashbacks still haunt him with the horrors of twenty-five years ago, but now we go through it together.

He is a kind, gentle man who lived through hell and it keeps coming back to haunt him. Over the years he's been spit on, laughed at, called a murderer, a baby killer and just plain crazy.

But to me, he will always be <u>MY HERO.</u>

Adele Lavigne - 1997

Nam Wife

A Nam wife,
confused …
about life.

Dealing everyday,
wondering …
will he stay?

Learning to cope,
knowing …
there is always hope.

Thinking of the time,
days …
when we are fine.

Someday he'll come home,
peace …
a life of our own.

Happy days are ahead,
thoughts …
as I go to bed.

Marie Leduc

Walking on Eggshells

My husband was in the Army – America 123rd Aviation Batallion in Chu Lia. He served from 1969-1971. He was in-country in 1970 and was Crew Chief, Door Gunner, E-4. He was shot in the knee by a sniper and hospitalized, but didn't receive the Purple Heart. At 17 he served in Korea and then Vietnam.

I work at home, have two children, both grown, and am a grandmother of two. My husband and I have been married for 19 years, and I am his fourth wife.

He exhibited symptoms of PTSD in 1979, nine years after his return. One of his main symptoms of PTSD is that he is very untrusting of everyone and thinks that they are out to get him. He was hospitalized in 1980 at the VA Hospital in Waco, Texas. Every three months he is in treatment … in psychotherapy. He is presently on Prozac and has been treated with many other medications. No one else in the family is being treated and we are very guarded and walk on eggshells. I have talked to the children and tried to help them understand.

My husband is 100% PT service connected, mainly due to PTSD and has a total knee implant.

My advice to others is never give up! I believe that is what the government wants you to do, but our vets are tired of fighting, so it is up to us to carry on this fight. My husband and I are active in many organizations, but mainly in the VFW. We are both officers in our local Post and Auxiliary at the District level. My vet may be getting an appointed position at the department level. He won 1st place at state this year for POW-MIA. That was quite an honor for us, especially due to the size of the state of Texas.

Lynn Richards

For Those Leaders
Who Will Listen

I want to forgive you and I want to thank you.

I want to forgive you for the thousands upon hundreds of us that were killed or maimed in Vietnam. I want to forgive you for the thousands we killed and all the homes, families and livelihoods that were destroyed – here in the U.S. – as well as in Vietnam. I want to forgive you and those responsible in our businesses and industries who knew we began turning over the outcome of that war to the Communists in the spring of 1968 and still kept spilling our blood and theirs for six more years. I want to forgive those who did not allow or tried to prevent the irresponsible nature of a self-centered South Vietnamese government to be respectfully and publicly presented which resulted in our country's gearing for the wrong "war" and therefore promoted the rise of conscientious activist who mistakenly lobbied for the "liberators" who buried a hamlet chief and his family alive, shot an 18-year-old girl to death while tied to a pole in her village center, assassinated a grandfather whose corpse fell pinning his two-year-old grandson to the ground, etc. I want to forgive our legalistic narrow-minded bureaucrats and our people who still do not understand. I want to forgive you for the constant searing pain. I want to forgive you for cutting me off from my family and friends and from helping the country and the world I love so dearly. I want to forgive those who hate me and those who do not care. I want to forgive you because I have learned to be forgiving myself.

And I want to thank you.

I want to thank you because your kind leadership has forced me to discover where no real answers are. Your subtle insanity (Eric Fromm was right) no longer demands my constant attention. No leaders from the east or west are going to "save" this world of and for people. I want to thank you for helping me understand you don't really want to lead, you want to be in the leadership position. Some of you want to control. I want to thank you because I had to learn that I must be conscious and responsible (response - able) for how I spend my time each day, not because of a need to demonstrate an accomplished final goal, but because the "how" I spend my days is not important. To be unselfish and not be afraid is my goal now, because of and in spite of your leadership. I want to thank you because you have this mere creature to accept my finite progressive humanity as a fact and now to hope you would begin to accept the fact that you are not God. Perhaps Gods, yes I unfortunately agree. God himself you would find does not play with truth, and would probably label secret decisions made for the "good" of a people as satanic or at least very sick.

Yes, I want to forgive. And I want to thank you.

But I can't

Yet!

Copyright Ed P. Ruminski 1981

Taken from *Beneath It All*

What Should I Do?

My husband was 18 when he served in Vietnam during 1968-1969. He was a private and served in a mechanized infantry unit. He never told me much about his tour in Vietnam or if he had any medals. I don't even know if he was wounded, but I do know that he is wounded in his mind.

He has been in a thirty-day intensive therapy treatment and has been hospitalized twice, once for suicide ideation and for depression.

Since I have known him he has exhibited symptoms of Post Traumatic Stress Disorder. He is presently in treatment attending weekly group sessions. He is taking antidepressants and sleeping pills.

Our family is not in treatment and there are no wives groups in our area. Closeness in the family is nonexistent. My veteran drinks, so I attend al-anon to learn how to cope. He is paranoid, jealous and an alcoholic. He is very critical of me, commenting on what I say or do. We have made no friends in the neighborhood since we moved in two years ago.

I work days and then he works nights, so there is very little family involvement. Most of the weekend he drinks and watches sports. I don't seem to exist unless he wants me to do something and then complains because I didn't do it right. I usually just get very quiet and leave him alone when he is drinking.

He puts on a front for his family, he is afraid that they will think he is a failure because we are in financial trouble. When he is with them he spends more money than we can afford and drinks excessively, so I have to drive home. Now I just refuse to go with him.

Our life is kind of crazy, sometimes I just feel like I should leave him! I just don't know what I should do!

JC

Didn't Say Much

Was talking to a vet, the other day,

Talked about the Vienam war.

Said, he didn't have much to say …

When we talked about Nam.

"I went to Nam!"

"I came home!" … "No big deal!"

"The worst that happened"

As his voice started to crack,

And almost got to a whisper,

"I lost a good buddy … over there!"

Tears filled my eyes, as I ended that call,

I could hear his anger and pain.

He didn't say much, yet he said it all …

When he talked about Nam.

Marie Leduc

He was only 20

My husband was in Vietnam in 1970-1971 for one year. He served with 1st of the 5th and the 25th units. As a door gunner his rank was E-4. He was awarded a Bronze Star, Army Flying Medal plus the normal medals given to Vietnam veterans. While being fired upon, his best friend was hit and died in his arms. He was only 20 years old when this happened. His uncle was also killed in Vietnam.

He first exhibited symptoms of PTSD, which include nervousness, panic, anger and withdrawal from society, after his return in 1971. He has been hospitalized for treatment once at the VA Hospital. He is in psychotherapy with a psychiatrist and visits once every three months, but occasionally talks with him on the phone. His various medications include proponanol and sleeping aids

Our family is concerned about his behavior, when he becomes nervous and anxious, or "going off" as they call it. Our family is not in treatment, but I have on occasion attended the treatment sessions. We don't go out as a family, he cannot tolerate crowds or loud noises.

I am afraid to sleep at night because of his nightmares when he fights, runs and kicks … hitting and kicking me on occasion.

Angie Raines

SCARED, SO SCARED...

TEARS IN MY EYES...

FEAR, FEAR CLOUDING MY THOUGHTS.

I WANT TO RUN...RUN WHERE?

HIS HAND REACHES OUT...

SOMEONE CARES!

I Have Become Educated About PTSD

My veteran served in Vietnam in 1967 along the DMZ with the 3rd Marine Division for 11 months. He was a 21-year-old sergeant assigned as combat engineer and participated in 13 operations. He was wounded with shrapnel in the head, back, and shoulder, but was not hospitalized.

After our son was born, he started exhibiting PTSD symptoms. He may have been exhibiting the symptoms before, but I may not have recognized them. He suffers from flashbacks, nightmares, social withdrawal, paranoia and psychotic breaks. He has been hospitalized seven times in both VA and civilian hospitals. In my opinion, his treatment has been poor, but he does see a psychotherapist twice a month.

His symptoms have affected the family tremendously. His social withdrawal affected the economic security of the family, causing us to go on welfare. His psychotic breaks caused emotional upheaval, loss of domestic tranquility, and involvement with the law, which led to arrest and institutionalization, and eventually the breakup of the family, after ten years of marriage.

My son had a psychotic break in his early 20s and was hospitalized. He is on medication and receives counseling, but he is currently stable. Our son and I are experiencing secondary PTSD and have gone through some family counseling based on our son's breakdown.

When we were still together and the more severe symptoms were manifesting, we went to counseling together and joined a support group for veterans and spouses. I attended counseling with him, but felt the need to separate our son from him. He was having severe flashbacks and losing touch with reality because his life was so chaotic. He distrusted everybody. At that time, I sought help from a counselor and the members of veterans support groups. Since then, I have become educated about PTSD, and have become a licensed psychotherapist, working with people who suffer from PTSD.

We got together when we were both in our mid twenties while in college. We resonated with each other to drop out of conventional society and left behind our conventional jobs and career paths. We did the "drop-out, tune-in (but, fortunately not too much of the) turn-on" trip. We bought property in northern Vermont, built a log cabin and grew a garden. After a year, we tired of the severe weather and moved in with his parents in New Jersey. Then we returned to my home in California and lived with my mother for a time while we got back on our feet financially. We moved north, to Mendocino County, where we bought property and built a cabin, living fairly primitively, without electricity or indoor plumbing.

He did start up a Heating and Air Conditioning business, but it failed when more severe PTSD symptoms hit him. We lived on welfare, and I worked part-time.

When he was first having symptoms and becoming disabled, we decided to move to Hawaii for some R&R. We moved rather impulsively, without jobs to go to. We traveled and looked for jobs but we were unsuccessful and out of money so we had to get bailed out by his family and return home. His PTSD symptoms got worse.

I initiated a separation and moved out of the house, but lived on the property. His flash-backs got worse and he had a psychotic break. Although we had been seeing a counselor and attending a support group, this was not enough to stabilize him. I was frightened by his psychotic behavior. He was not violent or abusive to either me or our son, but he was acting really crazy. I fled the property with my son and a neighbor called the police on him. When he resisted arrest it triggered him back to the war scene and he ended up incarcerated.

What he really needed was good mental health support, but he ended up criminalized. At that time, there was very little understanding of Vietnam veterans and Post Traumatic Stress Disorder. He eventually got some good help on the east coast and got VA disability. He is now stable, but lives a pretty isolated life in rural northern California.

Mary Delaney

When I Was 21

When I was 21
You went away.
My whole body ached for you
Arched for you
Cried for you
I was determined to die
If you died …
But they sent you back
Alive
A little changed
By what you'd been through
A little changed
Not much
At first
Thirty pounds lighter on your scrawny frame
And you couldn't sleep
But what the hell
You'd been in a war
Right?

So you couldn't sleep
And then you couldn't fly
You couldn't even walk sometimes
The dark dreams would clutch your heart so tight
Destroying your
Fragile
Hold on the world
Your heart stopped at night
Time after time
What shit he wrote
The valiant never taste of death but once
Did he fly into hot LZ's
Rescue wounded men because he was
too tired to give a damn and they needed him?

No.
You never once said no.
Till afterwards.
Then it was no
No
No
For years
To me
No.
It seemed like what ever I asked
The answer was no.

Still
Every once in a while
Maybe once a year
You would put your arms around me
Unasked
And whisper into the back of my hair
I do love you, you know

Patience Mason copyright 1989

81

Still In-Country

Only by meeting and falling in love with my husband did I learn how strong a person I actually could be. There can be many benefits to loving someone who still finds himself 'in-country' during 1969. I feel that our three children have many strengths that they would not have learned had they been raised by a so called 'normal' father.

I met my husband in '81, by this time he had already been diagnosed with an 'anxiety disorder.' PTSD was not a recognized condition then. He had already been 'kicked out' of two different VA hospitals for a noncompliance with their treatment programs and had lost his disability status. His personal treatment program for his problems was conveniently found in the bottom of many bottles. Since I met him at a community college, I did not know the extent of what I 'was in for' until after I had already begun to care about this wonderful person. My first battle was to get his disability reinstated. He was wounded while serving as a Marine 'in-county' and for some reason the VA determined he was well. Starting this battle was also a reason for him to 'self medicate' more often, hence the first of my strengths that he taught me. I had to fight the VA while keeping him sober enough to appeal their denials and go in front of their boards. We finally succeeded in having his original disability reinstated, and from there the battle continued.

When we met, I had two children and he had one, all of which we did manage to blend into one family. None of the three children could understand how the VA could say he was 'better' when the shrapnel in his body would set off every security check point we would go through, an airport, a courthouse, etc. We would have to stand and wait while he would have to take off his shirt, show his scars, etc. (Bear in mind this was way before the heightened security measures after 9/11/01.) The children were also aware of the nerve damage to his shoulder, his neck, his arm, his hand, etc. which is caused by this shrapnel. To this day we use only plastic cups and glasses since he never knows when his hand either will seize into a fist or to open completely causing him to drop what he may be holding. All of our children are now grown with homes of their own and keep 'special Dad glasses' for when he is there. Not only I, but all three of our children learned how to stretch the tendons and work on a person's hand until it is usable again. Little did we realize at the time that this would be our first lesson in physical therapy.

Once we had the original disability reinstated, then the real battle began. This time we went after the "PTSD" factor. I have lost count of how many times I have pulled him back from 1969, as have the children. They used to be afraid of waking him and would stand outside the door and call his name. I had to learn that 'special touch' and tone of voice with which to wake him. We all had to grow accustomed to his 'walking his perimeter' at 3:00 a.m. in the morning. We even managed to find humor in the fact that our animals would follow, which we referred to as 'helping him' while he would walk the fence line outside. Even today our grandchildren are used to their "Papaw" checking to make sure we are safe, and we have also passed the humor of the animals patrolling with him onto them. Yes, there are problems in dealing with someone who has PTSD, but the whole family has gone through counseling and has learned that this cannot be changed, only accepted. We have all learned the best way to accept this is to keep a sense of humor and just 'deal with it.'

Along with the 'patrolling' at different times came the fact that we never knew when a certain noise would cause him to pull the children under the dining room table in order to keep them safe. All three children learned to accept this, and to wait for me to use that 'special tone' in order to bring him back from '69. He has gotten better, but our children still know to look for his reaction during certain times. So far he has not felt this during any time our grandchildren were with us. The worst incidence of this was during a car wreck when they were trying to take our son on a 'chopper' to the hospital. He kept saying "if they take him we will never see him again." I was not there at the time, luckily one of the EMS workers was a 'Nam vet and knew what he was referring to. This 'brother' was able to convince my husband to let them take our son, and he even flew with our son after making a promise to my husband that he would make sure the boy was returned. I was told at the time that if my husband had not listened to this particular EMS person that he was to be 'restrained.'

After getting his VA benefits returned, and all of us going through plenty of counseling – individual and family – my husband actually became a DAV service officer. I feel that his helping other 'brothers' fight the system and receive what they deserve has helped him more than anything else. This finally gave him something to think about besides the 'ones he left behind.' The service he was giving to his brothers gave him a sense of helping his brothers instead of the feeling of desertion that he had carried for so many years. He actually fought with the medic while being loaded on the 'chopper.' He couldn't leave his brothers. By becoming a service officer he was helping and not deserting his brothers. In my opinion, and our children's, this job was better therapy than any counseling and/or treatment in a hospital that he ever received.

Speaking of VA hospitals, oh the joy you can incur while having a loved one there! Our children had to learn to accept the fact that most of the time if he was there, that was also where I stayed – especially since they all seem so far away from where we live. Of course during the PTSD hospital stays he would only be allowed visitors during certain week-ends after a certain amount of time. There have been other long term hospitalizations, tho'. He also has a disability connected to Agent Orange. In '97 he lost his right lung to Agent Orange, and the radiation treatment caused him to have a quadruple bypass in '02 (scar tissue on arteries). The children have learned to accept the fact that he may be a five-hour drive away for a major surgery and recovery, and that during the whole time I will be at that hospital. They have learned to accept the fact that at any time we may be on another long journey to another hospital for a long stay. They often encourage me to write a book on how someone can survive their loved one's stay at a VA hospital, all the 'ins and outs' and who to ask for what. One of the strengths I now recognize is that I can back a surgeon/specialist into a corner and find out exactly what is going on. I can fight to learn what they do not bother to tell my husband. I can also demand that they call me first when he is having problems with his PTSD, a VA hospital will put him back into 1969 faster than most other events. They will not restrain him when they can page me and I can bring him back with 'that touch' and/or 'that tone of voice.' Actually, once the staff learns that you WILL be present '24/7' they are usually more than happy to work with you, especially when they never know when you will 'pop up.' The worst thing they can do is tell you it isn't visiting hours and you have to leave. That's fine, and I saw what I needed to see.

There are so many things I could add because this could go on and on – we are talking about one person and the effect his experience 'in-country' during 1969 has had on at least three generations so far. Most of all he has made all of us stronger, more compas-sionate of what we may not know about someone else's life experiences, and that no one is perfect. Not all of our experiences have been 'good' or even 'easy,' but we are a closely knit family because of it. Our children learned early that everyone has baggage and that you have to accept the baggage if you want to love that person. This has helped them through their life relationships and life styles. My children did not learn to 'hate,' they learned to accept. My children learned patience, to give a person time and not judge by the first appearance. We have all learned that to make a family and to survive, each individual has to be their own person and part of the family. We learned there is a circle of life, which we are not only part of the big circle but make up our individual circles also. These are all lessons that not only myself and my children have learned, but which will also be passed down through generations. Living with a 'Nam vet can be difficult at times, but it definitely has benefits. Dealing with all his disabilities now and future will continue to be a learning experience for all of us … hopefully we can continue to make them positive ones.

For all of you out there who have a loved one with some similar or even different problems, just remember you are not alone. There is always someone ready to listen and to help.

Jacqueline McVicar

"His fight was in Vietnam,
Ours is the Vietnam in him."

Yoyo

Life with a PTSD veteran ...

UP

and DOWN

UP

and DOWN

      DOWN

        DOWN ...

It's all unraveling again ...

Wrap it up ... pull it tight,

    push me away

    pull me close

    push me away ...

    How long can we

    play this game?

Marie Leduc

Life is Up and Down With PTSD

My husband was stationed in Vietnam from 1968-1969. He served in Plieku, Ban Me Thout and Binh Phouc. He was an E-5 Sp/5 combat medic with 170th Assault Helicopter Company, 155th Assault Helicopter Company, Recon 2147th Infantry and 9th Infantry Division. He was awarded several bravery medals and a Purple Heart because he was wounded with shrapnel. When he served in Nam he was 19.

He exhibited symptoms of PTSD almost immediately after arriving home. He is presently in treatment, sees a counselor four times a month and participates in group therapy. He has been hospitalized in the VA and civilian hospitals.

Since he pretty much stays alone he does not affect the family too much. We try to be very encouraging to him since he has been up and down all of his life with symptoms of PTSD. The VA has been telling him that there was nothing wrong with him, but finally, after 32 years, they admitted that they were wrong and awarded him 100% service connected disability.

My first husband was a machine gunner with the first Marines. He was killed in action in 1968, leaving me a widow at 19 with our 13-month-old baby.

Anonymous

Memorial Day Toast

3 cheers for the 3 Musketeers ...

*1 beer for those who cared
and died for a lie ...*

*2 beers for those who cared
and still lie where they died ...*

*3 beers for those who came home, still
trying to understand why ...*

Memorial Day ...

How many really care for those who shed tears?

George R. Leduc

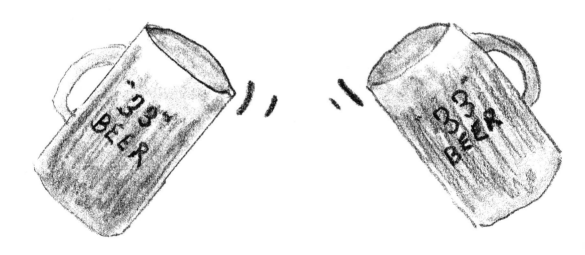

It Was a Godsend

My husband served in Vietnam in 1971 in Phu Bai with the army, attached to the 101st Airborne as a code breaker.

I met my husband when we were in high school. He and I dated briefly. We always seemed to date each other's best friends. We both ended up marrying those best friends. So we have quite a long history. I can say I knew him before and he was not the man who came home. He was a romantic who wrote poetry and loved nature. When he married his wife, she was an anti-war activist and said that she would divorce him if he wouldn't go to Canada. He couldn't do that. While he was in Vietnam, his wife divorced him. That was the straw that broke the proverbial camel's back. He attempted suicide and was shipped home. He was an inpatient at the Chelsea Naval Hospital for awhile and when they let him out on a pass, he came to see me. He was very different than the guy I had dated. I was four months away from getting married. We talked often and long about nothing but he seemed troubled … as if he wanted to tell me everything. He kept telling me that he wasn't right but couldn't explain it. The VA gave him a bottle of 500 valium, released him, and said to come back when the bottle was gone. He disappeared for awhile, but always came back to find me when he was in an emotional crisis. I heard stories about him all through the years, drugs, alcohol, and the craziness. For awhile he lived alone, like a hermit on a mountain in Vermont. He moved to Florida and was a waiter in Orlando. He took classes at a cooking school and became a chef. He met a woman and lived with her for 11 years and had sons with her, but never married her. After many years and a failed marriage, I ran into him again. We picked up where we left off and nine months later were married. The beginning was good. I didn't know what I was in for so I guess ignorance was bliss. He had just been released from the VA detox unit. He was in intensive therapy and on major pharmaceuticals! He hid most of it from me. He didn't even tell his shrink that he was married. Then things started to fall apart. The drinking was back with a vengeance and so was the drugging … all prescription. He would get violent, although he never hurt any of us. The anger in him was tremendous. The lies, the deceit, the feeling of utter helplessness, the times he would call me from the road and say he was taking off for awhile … all of it was horrific. I was sure I could make him better. I tore myself apart trying. This went on for two years, and it was getting worse with each passing day … for him and for me. Then we found out he had Hepatitis C from Vietnam – another gift from the Orient. He tried Interferon for the first time about two years after we were married. The series of shots and meds literally almost killed him …

of course he was still drinking at that time and denying it. The first round failed. More despair for all of us. The "magic" day that saved our lives was also the worst day of our lives. He was VERY drunk and went to get his son. He called me and was abusive and nasty but assured me he was okay to get him. His son was nine at the time. He ended up getting pulled over and arrested. His PTSD reared its ugly head when they locked him up. While I was on the phone with the police, I could hear him screaming like a caged animal. At that point I was ready to divorce him. I asked the police officer if I could try to get him into the VA and I thank my higher power, he said okay. I called and arranged for him to be admitted from the jail. The police officer listened when I told him to let my husband exhaust himself before he should talk to him. I explained that he had PTSD and even though the officer didn't really understand … he did as I asked. Dwight was in the VA for three days before he called me. He told me to divorce him while I could. Instead, I went to the hospital and met with him and his doctors. He had court the next day, but I wouldn't go. They took him in and he was allowed, again, I think thanks to the arresting officer, to go to a halfway house in New Bedford, MA for Vietnam vets. It was a God-send. There he got sober and clean. He learned humility and that he had a disease that would be with him forever. He learned that he had a family that loved him and he would lose it if he did this again. He was there for six months and lost his license for three years. So I was punished too … I had to do ALL of the driving. He went back to school and got his bachelors degree in 2003. And hopefully in the fall he will graduate with his masters. He is going to be a therapist who deals with PTSD patients and with all the men coming back from Iraq, he will have a purpose. I know he still has major issues. Every once in a while they will surface and scare me. And at random times too. Usually something small will set off a memory. He never really talks about Vietnam with me. Sometimes he will relate a memory, but usually it is when he has had an "Episode." Then it is an epiphany for him … me too. There are so many more stories about this. I could fill a hundred pages. Good times and very bad ones. I never had to worry about him sleeping with a knife or hurting me as many wives of PTSD patients do. His was always more psycho-logical damage that was done. I am forever different because of this. I am stronger and more self-reliant. At the same time, I am more cautious and observant. I "walk the perimeters" of my mind every day, keeping myself safe and strong so I can be ready for whatever comes next. One of the best things that has happened recently is that he went through another round of Interferon and this one worked. He is virus free and has been for a year and a half. He goes for his final test soon and if that is clear, and all indications are that it will be, he will be cured. One life sentence commuted. The other ever present and waiting. And the ultimate irony is that neither one was of his own doing. He did what he was told to do … but you take it one day at a time and at the end of the evening, you thank your higher power for getting through another one and prepare for the next. I try to be supportive and as patient as I can … NOW … before it was very different. I was always anxious and worried. I thought I could "cure him." I love my husband. I tell him "you have to walk through the mud to get out of the swamp and I will be there with hip waders to walk with you." I know I am one of the few lucky ones.

Dianne

My Goal

Some days are good, some are not ...

Is it because of the war I fought,

so far away in another land?

What can I do to understand?

Another year, time goes by ...

But, I'm still asking why,

why do I dream such dreams at night?

What can I do to end this fight?

I want peace, I want a life ...

My family, friends and my wife.

To get out of this black hole,

to have happy days is my goal!

Marie Leduc

It is Frightening

Being the wife of a veteran with PTSD can be scary with a lot of tension. The children think he is grumpy and mean and try to isolate themselves from him. I go to meetings for spouses and that has helped me understand PTSD better. He also goes to group once a week to help with his depresson, anger and fears. He has suicidal thoughts while trying to deal with flashbacks, dreams, and night sweats.

He served mainly in Tay-Ninh and Cu-Chi with the 588th Engineers as a heavy equipment truck driver.

His PTSD started in 1976, but at the time he didn't have a name for what was causing so many of his problems. Today, knowing what PTSD is, it can still be frightening at times and the family still walks on eggshells.

Wanda Miley

The Awakening

When I awoke from my slumber
I felt the morning
sun against my face.

As the sleepiness left my being
I felt the surrounding
warmth caress, of the sun

I could feel the tingling
of its warmth surround me,
and I floated into the sky to meet it.

From this warm feeling as my body awoke
more and more
the smell in the air was of musk scent?

And not the sweet smell
of a spring morning but a
confusing aurora of sound.

As the sounds came alive around me,
I heard a Voice, "Move Out!"
This is what I heard.

Then I realized I was not home
but in a war,
not for God and country, but within myself.

I then knew the beauty I saw now
is just a long lost memory,
that lingers on.

But the feeling lives on and on
deep inside of me.
and searches for a man that will never be!

A piece of the turmoil that embraces me
and sends me afar, to a place that has no time,
no day or night ... a place to die.

Like the chill of a fall morning as the leaves
slowly fall to the earth,
then so must I, fall to the earth,
so one day I can float into the sky.

To a new life of peace ...

Alex F. Gordaoff

Sadness

My husband was stationed in Vietnam in 1968-1969 … total time in-country was one year. He was an operating room technician, Spec 5 and was assigned as a field medic at a Battalion Aide Station in the operating room. He served in Can Tho, Mc Tho and 9 ID Mekong Delta. He served at the age of 19 and 20. He received the standard Vietnam service medal plus a Bronze Star and a Purple Heart.

It was 14 years after his service that he exhibited symptoms of PTSD, the main one being depression. Other symptoms are sleep apnea, insomnia, anxiety, restlessness, lack of concentration, poor memory and recall, headaches, irritability, rage, increased hostility with colleagues and family members. In addition he has night terrors, confusion, bewilderment, sedentary life style with weight gain. He has poor nutrition, inadequate stress management, and poor coping skills. He is in complete denial and he rationalizes about his situation. He is completely withdrawn from society and is disassociated from family and friends. In 1997 he had suicide ideation twice and I was not sure if he had a plan as there were no apparent attempts.

He had difficulty keeping positions as a physician and he was unable to practice medicine for two years. He was hospitalized twice for psychiatric reasons. He has been diagnosed with major depression and is bi-polar, making him unable to return to work for awhile, but he sees his psychiatrist once every three weeks for medication.

Our family has been affected severely trying to cope with our situation. I am in treatment for major depression and we have two sons with bi-polar in treatment. We have been married for 32 years but I feel sad that my life has been wasted living with a zombie. He refuses to address the issues affecting his life, mine and the children. He has inflicted severe damage to people who are now estranged from him and he doesn't understand why. During a recent holiday family visit, he scared my family and I insisted that he say something to them in the way of an explanation and then call his doctor or I would, with or without his permission. He made no comment. When I called his physician he suggested immediate contact with his sleep doctor and made an adjustment in his prescription for night terrors. He refused to take the medication.

I am very angry with him for not getting help. This is an educated man and a trained physician. I live with a man who screams every night in his repressed rage. I just don't know how we will end up!

Anonymous

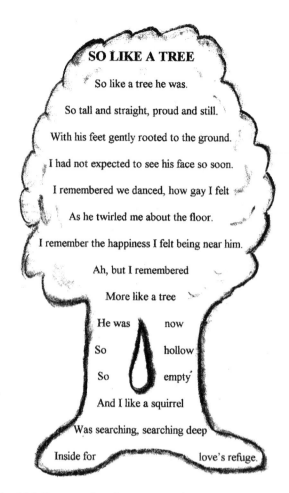

SO LIKE A TREE

So like a tree he was.

So tall and straight, proud and still.

With his feet gently rooted to the ground.

I had not expected to see his face so soon.

I remembered we danced, how gay I felt

As he twirled me about the floor.

I remember the happiness I felt being near him.

Ah, but I remembered

More like a tree

He was   now

So   hollow

So   empty

And I like a squirrel

Was searching, searching deep

Inside for   love's refuge.

When I was a girl of 15, I wrote the above poem for creative writing class. Many years later I added the words "more," "now," and "love's" to refuge. When I wrote the poem as an "extended simile," it was originally about the shallowness of the boys I knew. Years later, living with a Vietnam veteran, it became about the changes in him. I continued to search and seek out the refuge of his love for me that was formed before he went to a place that forever changed him. It is that love that has been my solace in times that are filled with bad memories. It is that hidden love, that surfaces now and then, that has been hope and strength that has kept me at his side through almost 36 years of marriage. It is that love, that fills his soul and keeps him ever battling the guilt of being one of the few survivors of a battle where he sustained injuries during an explosion, was shot while lying waiting for help and then was mistaken for dead and thrown on a pile of bodies. This is his story more than it is mine. A story of uncelebrated duty and honor. The story of a Vietnam veteran who shall always be a hero in my eyes.

Jade Rivis

Pathway to Love

I met Jim in 1966, at a restaurant where we worked. I was sixteen and he was nineteen. When I first met Jim, I absolutely disliked him. I hated his wiseguy antics and how he constantly teased me, and I did not want to have much to do with him. My mom, who also worked there, was always trying to fix me up with him and I didn't appreciate that either. I have long since realized that I was blessed to hate all his bad qualities, long before I discovered and loved all his good ones. Perhaps that pathway to love is more realistic than most and has been the reason our marriage has lasted so long. One can only guess at those things.

We worked together closely enough for me to observe that he did not act the same way with the people he knew better. It was then that I observed that he was basically shy with strangers, and his wise-cracking, teasing way was to mask that shyness. I also noticed that with the guys and with the older women, he was well thought of and did not act the same way as he did toward me. His shyness was acute when it came to girls close to his own age. My heart began to soften toward him as I got to know him better so I took it upon myself to educate him. If he would just be himself, he would have nothing to worry about with girls (yes, I was rather smug in my day). As we became friends I was treated to a view of a young man deeply sensitive to others and so shy of girls that he did not date much. Since I did not drive, he began giving me a ride home, and we would sit for hours and just talk. Somewhere in the midst of this friendship were the beginnings of romance. When he asked me out on a date, I really think he thought I was going to say no, but I agreed and we began to date.

I guess you could say we went steady. We exclusively dated each other from September of 1966 to May of 1967 when he entered the Marine Corps. Our relationship after that was ongoing, but not exclusive. The Marine Corps training had given him a new assurance of himself. He went into basic training a boy and came out a man. More than that, he was a man that I could love, and did love with all my heart. I loved him enough to be there for him when he needed me or step back when necessary. I guess you might say that I felt like our story was "to be continued" at the other side of Vietnam.

You see, Jim knew Vietnam was inevitable as a destination, and, to put it delicately, I was not into the sexual revolution that was happening around me. When I caught him in a lie, having seen him with another girl, I told him I did not own him. It was not like we were engaged – he did not have to lie – just say he had another engagement. I loved him dearly, and was hurt by it, but also understood that he felt there was a possibility of not coming back and wanted to experience all he could. Neither of us really spoke about the possibility of not surviving Vietnam. I for one prayed for that not to happen. He did not want to think about it. So, I was content to see him when I could, and tried not to hold him back from "sowing his oats" as my mom used to put it.

As a Scout dog handler in Vietnam, he was assigned to units by need and mission. He walked point, with the dog ever on the alert. There was some resistance to the ability of the dogs. He wrote to me about it. He also wrote that the enemy did not have the same resistance and that in fact had put a price upon his head, and the head of his dog. Jim was not in country long. His memories are a big foggy. Walking point, they ran into enemy fire and he was trying to get up a hill to get a better view, when a large blast came from behind. It sent him flying head over heels and looking at devastation, as a second blast went off and the shrapnel from that burrowed into his left arm. As he watched that hot metal and realized the first blast had done damage, he noticed that his dog was gone and he thought he had been killed. He wondered if he and the dog had set off the blast and if he had missed the dog's alert, but, he realized, it all had happened so fast, that by the time the dog would have alerted, the blast came.

As he laid waiting for the medic, he was being shot at by a sniper. He crawled to a tree, and used it for cover, but the sniper was still able to shoot him in his exposed side. The round went through his waist and took his intestines out with it. I guess he passed out for a bit but he remembers someone laying him down, checking for a pulse and not being able to move at all. Whether that was the result of the shrapnel that had burrowed into his hips and spine, or shock, he does not know. The next thing he remembers is the feeling of floating, hitting something soft, and opening his eyes to realize that he was on a pile of dead bodies. The marines load the dead first, and then the wounded, so he remembers thinking … I must be dead. He had no further thoughts until the tail gunner was pulling him off the pile and calling the medic. As the medic took a rag, wet it from his canteen, put it on his intestines and pushed them close against him … he was thinking that maybe I'm not dead after all.

He did not admit it until years later, but, he also questioned – why not? Somehow he felt responsible for the blast and felt he had not adequately done his job. Over the years, he began to think of that day, and felt that all the men that had died were because of him. The more prejudice against Vietnam veterans he encountered, the more he retreated to that place of hidden misery and grief and the more he blamed himself for the events of that day. The more society disparaged the Vietnam veteran, the worse he felt about himself and his service. The worse he felt, the more he felt guilty about living through the experiences. All this was not revealed for many years.

The only hint in the early years of our marriage about PTSD was the nightmares, and one occasional statement I heard him say, "Better men than me died in Vietnam." I knew nothing of PTSD, because Jim did not associate with veterans, except those who were cops along with him, and they never discussed Vietnam. Not ever. He would barely admit he was there. The treatment at home of the veterans was enough to shut their mouths. Being spit on, while at home on convalescent leave, had been enough for him not to even wear the uniform except on base and to and from work. The once proud marine was shrouded by a cloud of malice, which withered him to that tree that was hollow and empty and a place of wearing a shell of pride that no longer truly meant anything to him. In the place of retreat was a desire to push everyone away, and not let them close enough to see that vast hurt.

Looking back now, I see the signs and symptoms that followed us, everywhere we lived. In 35 years of marriage, we have had 23 different addresses, and have lived in four states. We used to camp a lot. Somehow now I see that as a balm for his soul. Something that helped him to hold on, for so long, to life, and work, and love. His first crisis with PTSD came shortly after he turned 30. Suddenly a desire to see some of the fellows he went through Scout Dog training school with became a burning desire. He did track them down, and had them over for a weekend reunion, and they talked about it all. There were tears and laughter, and a lot of drinking and cursing and "male bonding." One of the two friends was married and his wife and I basically hung out together with the kids and just stayed out of their way. That weekend was the first time he found out his dog had survived that day, and had gone on to another handler. But all the memories were too much for him, he became suicidal, and refused any help but mine. That was when he told me about his desire to go to Oregon, and I agreed to sell everything and go. Crisis averted? I see now it was just delayed. Part of me just thought he was being overdramatic with the suicide thing, and that he was using it as an excuse. Now that I look back, I remember that in revealing to me some of the pain, he was relieved I did not run away from him, and recoil at the ugliness he felt lived inside.

A few months back, he had read an article on Vietnam veterans living in the woods of Oregon and Washington state. He had passed it on to me to read. I just had this feeling that if I did not go with him to Oregon, he too would disappear in the woods with these vets. Our son was four years old, no school to hold him, so I said, "Let's go." Both our families looked at us like "strangers from another planet." I have always been close to my mom and family, our best friends were his older brother, who was also a police officer, and his wife. All of them tried to talk him out of going ... to no avail. Some wanted me to stay behind, but I could not.

The one person that could have probably talked him out of it was his dad. However, he was deceased. Jim's dad had passed away shortly after we returned to New Jersey when Jim got an early out of the marines as so many were coming back and there was no room to station them all. Perhaps that loss was greater to him than he would admit. His dad was the one person he did discuss the war with. His dad had been a World War II marine, and had been stationed at Pearl Harbor the day it was bombed. As I look back and see the symptoms, I see those "if only" as well. If only I had known about PTSD then, I would have gotten him to the VA for help. If only his dad had been there, I could have enlisted his help. Sorrow usually follows those "what ifs" and I have had to stop myself too many times to count from giving in to them. The PTSD escalated through the years, and I did not recognize it, because I did not know about it. That leaves me with some guilt as well.

The move to Oregon worked to calm him for a bit. When he encountered trouble breaking into law enforcement there, he went to Alaska for a job interview on a small, isolated island. When I made him see that as too much of a hardship for his son, he decided we should go back to New Jersey. You see, Jim had two ambitions in life—to be a marine and to be a police officer. Being a police officer was an essential part of his living. As a police officer, he could continue to live in life-and-death situations, a parody of "in-country" feelings of Vietnam. Being a police officer had a way of both making you feel you were doing something important, and supplying the adrenaline rush of living life on the edge. Edge of what? Death, my friends. The underlying part of all his symptoms that I did not see was his death wish.

We were not back in New Jersey long before the wanderlust returned. Another police officer had moved to Florida, and in a desire for company, sent him an application for a city police force near Ft. Lauderdale where he was working, and it started all over again. Before I knew it, we were on the road to Florida, this time armed with school transfers for our son. He and his friend worked together for a year. Their goal was to obtain their certification and then go to a County Sheriff's office. I had not realized how Jim's behavior was affecting our son, until he had an accident with his bicycle that injured another child and he hid, and was afraid to tell his dad. Jim's friend found him hiding, brought him home and explained the situation. Jim stood by his son, and when the friend was accepted by one Sheriff's department, but Jim's first offer was from another, Jim took that first offer to give our son a new start.

He worked hard at trying to mend the relationship. PTSD just has a way of getting in the way of all the best intentions. I give him a lot of credit for pushing himself to do things our son liked in order to spend time with him. Our son may, however, remember only the impatience and anger when things did not go right. I tried often to explain, but I could see the hurt in our son's eyes, which would not let him see what I was trying to impart. Jim's body began to give him a lot of trouble, from wounds to shrapnel, pain was increasingly a problem. The doctor who performed the sciatic nerve surgery had told him that it would last 15 years, and the pain began to attack his mental ability. He was determined, however, to keep working as a police officer, so he began going to the VA.

Along with this was the shrapnel which was embedded in his spine and hip joints, shifting and making it painful to do even the simplest parts of law enforcement. Pushing your body in healthy condition is one thing, but pushing it with the various problems of past injuries, to me takes a lot of strength. Jim has always been my hero, even in the worst of times. He was so bad at one point the VA had to give him an electrical unit to wear to block the pain. The pain also put an extra drain on his emotional and mental health. The distractions, as well as the pain, started the memories of that day, over and over again. He had suppressed so much, that I feel the pain was like a gate in the fence, opening up and letting the memories flood out.

The next crisis with PTSD came when Jim had a flashback while on a manhunt. The terrain in the area of the search reminded him of Vietnam. It was night, and the only light was the moon, and suddenly he was back in Vietnam. He talked with the pastor at our church about it, but he had no idea how to deal with it and told Jim that it was an isolated incident and not to worry. (I knew nothing of all this until after his hospitalization for PTSD years later.) I think the pastor may have thought it was the alcohol that caused it, and he was praying for Jim so I shall not hold him to blame for believing his prayers would be helpful. After all, pastors are human too.

The flashbacks continued. Jim was promoted to the detective bureau and he jumped at the chance to get off the road. He was afraid of shooting someone while in a flashback. I sit and shake my head at the rolling events now, and say, how could you not see? I can find no excuse for myself. By that time Jim was what I call a "functional alcoholic." That is to say, he did not drink on the job or before the job, but he did drink before going to bed every day. He tells me it was "self medicating" to get rid of the nightmares and flash-backs. Now I see it clearly. Then, I was just mad about the abuse of alcohol.

Still there were times that the old Jim came through and romanced me, and sent me flowers and loved me fully. Those times were becoming less and less frequent, however, now that I look back at it with a clearer eye. It was the "alcohol" that I blamed, and really that was another symptom. Our son went with a friend to the teen group of the family of alcoholics for awhile, in order to try to understand, which I encourage. As far as help, I am afraid that was all that he had, except for me, constantly telling him it was not his fault.

The stress in the detective bureau was even greater than on the road. There was more time at the desk than with road work. Jim felt cooped up, on top of it all. Another detective got him Valium under the table. He began living what he calls a "double life." The competent detective with an eye for detail, that had an arrest/conviction rate of 98 percent, and the jelly fish person he became the moment he left that role. He put himself totally into the job, working more and more hours, answering calls meant for his partner, and burning himself out. Then one day, when he walked into an autopsy he was assigned to cover because of an unattended death of an older woman, it all hit him like a ton of bricks. The woman was a waitress at the restaurant where we met, and he recognized her. All that stuff he had been detaching himself from, Vietnam, the police experiences, came home to roost on his overburdened mind, which was trying to manage both physical and mental pain.

Shortly thereafter, on his birthday, he took all the money he could out of the joint bank account, booked himself a flight, left a letter of resignation and his guns in his briefcase in the trunk of his plainclothes police car at the station house and ran away. When tracked down by his buddies on the police force, it was found that he had gotten a ticket to California. At that moment I knew he was headed north to Oregon and Washington. Alone, he would either flee to the woods and live out his days in seclusion, or he would be fleeing there for a peaceful place to die. By the grace of God, he would be landing in a city where a school friend lived, which his younger brother had kept in contact with. The police there would do nothing but stop him and ask him if he needed help. But the buddy could give him a haven.

The buddy, a Vietnam veteran, was a medical professional and knew all about PTSD. How thankful I am that Gary was there to meet him. He took him home with him, and convinced him to go to the VA hospital. Gary gave him all he needed. Gary's wife was

Vietnamese and she and Jim and Gary exorcised a lot of memories. Gary took the time and care, despite his own battle with cancer, which has since taken his life. I shall ever be in debt to him. After outpatient treatment and a lot of talking, Jim was returned to me in Florida, to enter the PTSD treatment in Miami as an inpatient. I was not allowed to see him for awhile. But I left there armed with every publication they had available. I saw what I had not seen, and by the time he came home I was a little bit equipped to help him.

Still my hero, he was determined that he would get through this place of doom that threatened to swallow him. He began the outpatient treatment. He joined a group therapy session in a storefront in West Palm Beach. There at the group, he met a man who had been at the same battle where he had been hurt. This man assured Jim he was not at fault, telling him that it was discovered that an enemy soldier had set off two 500 pound bombs just as the main force reached where they were. There would have been no survivors at all if the second one had not only had a delayed blast, but it had only exploded one quarter of its potential. Those in the back part of the unit had been spared a lot of the devastation as it exploded in a forward motion, towards those victimized by the first blast. Even with this information, his guilt, which he had held onto for so long, still often made him feel responsible.

The West Palm group often had family days with outings like picnics or parties at the center. My son and I attended and made some friends. Having someone to help us through was a bonus. Whether this was exclusive to this group, or a program that was later dropped, I do not know. I only know that this pattern did not continue when we moved back to NJ. I wonder sometimes if moving back here made things harder for him. Sometimes it is hard not to take blame for some of what he has endured.

Jim got himself a job as a credit manager for a welding company under a VA program. He managed to work tied to a desk for over a year, before it became too much for him. He quit the job and stayed home awhile, sinking again into the PTSD woes, as I call them. The owner of the business where he had worked had taken a liking to him, and tried to get him to come back. He was really good at the job, but he could never see himself in a "desk job" and felt trapped by it. By this time we had long since left the camping behind. If I could have gone back and changed anything, I think it would have been to continue that. The owner offered Jim a job selling and delivering on the road, and he took it and went back to work for him doing that. The variety was more helpful to him, and having something to do was a discipline that helped him get back some control. Also, under my insurance he was able to go to a pain management course, which helped him at that end.

At the same time that I lost my job my sister came for a visit and told me that my mom was having problems making ends meet since my dad's death. I felt very vulnerable and all I wanted to do was go home. I could find a job as easily in New Jersey, and my mom needed me. Jim could have said no, and probably should have, but he figured he owed it to me I guess. So, we sold our house, and moved back to New Jersey. He found work in security and I found work in my career. He had another crisis ten years later. I sometimes wonder if bringing him back was the cause. However, I have come to realize that almost a pattern of crisis every ten years has been the status quo of this creature called PTSD.

The breakdown of his body, and no longer having to maintain "top physical condition," may have been a catalyst to his next crisis. Possibly the way he was treated by people he used to call friends may well have been another. He reached a place where "you cannot understand," which became a place of "so why should I even listen to you." I do not blame anyone. It may have been nothing other than a natural progression of the disease. I just wonder if the "exclusiveness" of the program at the VA clinic may not have contributed to the nature of his next crisis. Anger was now being vented against those who "could not understand." That included me. I could no longer be the best friend I always was. He no longer even really listened to me … he heard me … but he did not listen. I became this outsider who could not understand.

This time the crisis was directed outward towards a boss, rather than against himself. No violence occurred since he was still in treatment; it was caught before it was a full blown incident. Once or twice I had to drive him to the group, because of car problems or something, I do not even remember now, and heard a bit of what was being discussed. Lately he has not had a desire to go to the group, and I really am not that upset. While I understand that anger and resentment of treatment over the years should be exercised, and maybe it is just time for that in the cycle of the disease, I am having more difficulty than at any previous time, because I have been the "enemy" in his eyes for quite a few years now. I wonder if it is true, or if it is imagined.

The progressive departure from my being his helper, his friend, was so gradual that I did not notice it for many a year. When recommendations for his not working came, I faced it with trepidation. Knowing that his value as a human being had always been tied to work, I feared a greater decline and a return to alcohol. Perhaps my fear, which became a delayed reality, coupled with the fact that I was no longer "listened to," has been a contributor to the decline of what used to be an ever-present faith. Perhaps I have just gotten worn out. All I know is that for the last six years, I myself have been declining into depression and despair. Is this a side effect of his PTSD? I sure hope not. However, I have realized that when I was an inspiration to him and a help, I never gave in to hopeless thinking. Now I feel helpless … all I am able to do is stand by and watch. The delay to his decline? My mom's need for a "watcher".

Jim had always loved my mom as his own. When her mental health began to decline to the point where she could not remember even the simplest things, like even occasionally where she lived, he became dad to her. He handled the problem better than any of her children could. He gave her the freedom she clung to so dearly, while watching and caring from afar. He would let her take her walks, always making sure he knew where she was going, and when she was gone too long, could reel her in with a joke and a lunch date. We just wanted her to quit doing what she had always done, to protect her. I guess that in his own way Jim understood mom better than we did. While our living with her caused some friction as it always would, helping mom gave him purpose. Purpose helped him to fight against the PTSD woes.

I marvel at the way he handled things with mom. I envied his patience. Jim was mom's friend, before he was my friend, my love. Jim was always the favorite son. Heck, mom always took his side in any argument. I have to laugh at that. It used to make me so angry. Hey mom, I am your daughter, am I not entitled to have you on my side? No, I was not, because Jim could not be wrong. Jim was still that Jim in mom's eyes that she knew before Vietnam. It made me look for that Jim … seek him out a lot more. Maybe my mom's mental state, remembering yesteryear, and not being able to remember yesterhour, was more help to me in dealing with Jim's PTSD than even I realized. She was always making me remember who he is, deep down in his core, the man I fell in love with. As many times as I have thought to give up on my Jim, my mom's view was always a help to me. Living with her and taking care of her was taxing and tiring, but helpful too. Jim never changed for my mom. That is nice to know. I think that was helpful to him too. He was the Jim she loved so well, and he lived up to her expectations.

The results make me acutely aware of the prejudice. Why is it that I see so many of these things that no one else seems to see? Has living with someone with PTSD given me insight, or paranoia? I truly wonder sometimes. Is my view warped? Or is it based more in reality, because of the reality of PTSD and its effects?

I was taught that we should forgive and forget and that meant that you do just that. I find that what the bible actually says is that you forgive, and forget the debt. The offense itself should never be forgotten, or it will not be avoided in the future. I forgive the offense against the Vietnam veteran. I will not hold it against anyone. But I will not forget that offense, nor allow it to reoccur against my son. Yet so many can, and are doing just that. To allow a teacher to talk to a child regarding a serving veteran in the manner that Vietnam veterans were spoken of and to is an atrocity. More atrocities are being formulated against Vietnam veterans than were ever performed by a few in each and every action or war. Those atrocities continue today, to our current generation of serving military, by people opposed to the current war. Those few, by the way, which come in each generation, are responsible for all the crimes that exist, and more of them do not go into military service than those that do. If you have to hate something, I would like to say, hate evil not people and do not attach evil where it does not dwell.

I would like to think that my standing by Jim made a difference in his fight against PTSD. In fact, the VA turned him down the first time for his rating of PTSD, because "he has been married for 20+ years," penalizing him for having a Christian wife who honored the vows. If I am totally honest, the best I can say is that I have been an anchor to the boat of his life. A little too lightweight to hold him fast in the really big storms. I remember feeling like I was being dragged along the bottom through the mud a few times. But I have "hung in there," because the man he was surfaces enough to pull me in the boat and hug me close. So, I cannot take credit for a mutual relationship of love and care. If he had not held up at least a part, I do not think I would have survived the trip. The strength to resist is from a larger source than "little old me." I am not afraid to say, "Thank you, God". You formed a man with strength, courage, and wit that would forget all the world would throw at him. And you formed him just for me. There is one thing I can say without any doubt, life has never been boring or predictable with my Jim. I would not trade the things I have done and seen, for anything except Jim never having to go through all that he has gone through. PTSD may well have accentuated the negatives, but it cannot and should not eradicate the positives. How much of PTSD is the effect of the trauma is argumentative as well. Other Vietnam veterans have had comments and prejudice, that he could not have PTSD, he wasn't there that long. That boggles my mind. That one veteran could put down another because, "I saw more bad stuff than you could ever see in that short time." "Hey dude," I want to say to that person, "He Lived That Stuff You Saw!"

I cannot imagine the type of strength it takes to get through the experience my Jim had to. Do I understand PTSD? No way. Why does it occur in one and not another? I do not have any answers, except perhaps it has to do with personal experiences, that either feed it, or starve it. The fact that PTSD has been around and called by many different names does not explain it, it simply identifies that the human mind's fragile balance can be influenced by traumatic experience. The truth is, that many scoff at PTSD, or deny that it is real … yet they display a lot of signs and symptoms of it. PTSD is a monster, a boogey man that we really do not want to face. But when we do, we find it is nothing more than a shadow, gone awry in human imagination. It will take many shapes and forms, so you must train yourself to live with it, and use it, rather than let it use and abuse you.

Jade Ravis

"You and Me"

Just kids,

went to war,

became men.

You and me … in Vietnam

Things we saw,

we heard,

we experienced

You and me … in Vietnam

Flying low,

brothers on the ground,

fighting Charlie.

You and me … in Vietnam

Some are home,

some are not,

some in a box.

You and me … coming home

Left my gifts,

my prayers and tears,

left a part of …

Me and you … at "The Wall"

Marie Leduc

Best Friends

Mike and I met while we both were working for SWBT. He was newly divorced from his 2nd wife with whom he has two sons. He and his first wife have a daughter. When we decided to get married and were looking for a house, he told me to find a house without any windows. I thought he was out of his mind, but I was able to find one that only has a window in each room, which are always locked and the curtains pulled. Our doors are always kept locked. We have a gun or knife in every room, with ready access for him to get to, but not on display for other people to get a hold of.

I am a person who likes to speak her mind and argue from time to time. This didn't set well at all with Mike, in fact it is one of the few things that caused problems between us. Instead of Mike arguing or hurting me he would put me in a headlock, drag me to the kitchen sink and hose me down with cold water until I would shut up or go limp. After a few months of going places with a wet head I went to the doctor and was put on Prozac to help curtail my outbursts. I have learned over the years to watch my mouth, try not to argue and keep a lot of stuff buried inside.

One night during one of his many nightmares, Mike bent our iron headboard and ended up crouched on the floor. That was when I truly realized something was wrong. The boys and I always felt like we were walking on eggshells because we never knew what was going to set him off or when. Sometimes it'd be the littlest thing. During the day we would have to announce who it was coming through the door so as not to take him by surprise. Mike is a very light sleeper, so when the boys were dating and came in late they would announce at the door who was coming down the hall, so they wouldn't get shot. Sometime later I was watching a TV program about a rape victim when they mentioned PTSD and gave some of the symptoms, which set off a light bulb in my head as to what our problem was. I started researching all the information I could find about PTSD and began to see a lot of the symptoms in Mike.

Mike likes animals and kids, but only tolerates grownups. He is a great provider and was very active with the boys growing up. He coached them in every sport they participated in. Mike and I are each other's best friend. We do everything together and he is definitely a family person.

I have always picked at him and encouraged him to talk about his experience in Vietnam, because I knew that would be part of his healing process. He has to sit with his back to a wall where he can see the entrance to the door at home and in public. If he had his way he'd never leave the house. He doesn't like crowds so when we are out I have to stay close by his side.

When I finally was able to convince Mike to go to the VA to get help, he found out in group that he wasn't in this world by himself. He thought the guys were talking about him at first, but he then realized they were telling their own stories. At the VA he was given what we call "By God" pills, because "By God" if he doesn't take them, all hell could break loose. Life began to be livable for us and all those around him. I talked Mike into going to a Vietnam Chapter meeting and he has been actively involved ever since. We are now Service Officers trying to help other vets get what is due them.

I have a form of OCD which causes problems between us because I am a saver of things and Mike is a neat and orderly person. He offers to help me get rid of my items but each time it makes me sick to my stomach because his way of helping is to burn the stuff. There are still times when he gives me an ultimatum on different things he feels needs to be done, and when he does that I feel like the child and he's the Dad.

He has asked many times over the years why didn't he die in Nam? I told him that God wasn't finished with him then. That God had a purpose for him and he'd never know what that purpose was until God called him home. I thought the time was near when Mike had 5-way bypass surgery, but thankfully he is still with us.

We have had a good 25 years of marriage, full of learning, love, ups and downs, as it was a great learning experience for both. We are looking for another 25 plus years if the Lord sees fit. I wouldn't trade him for anyone else and thank the Lord every day for letting me be by his side to help him.

Jo Callahan

Wife of a Vietnam Veteran
and Proud of It

Courage

Courage is emotions, we never felt before …

laughter, fear, anger, trust and tears,

letting go of feelings

we have kept in all these years.

Courage comes throughout our life,

in many different ways …

finding feelings in our heart,

as we learn to understand

it is not the end, but really just a start.

Courage is not something, you keep just for yourself …

but, something that you share,

it is a gift, the gift of love,

of showing someone else you care.

Marie Leduc

Loneliness ... and Courage

Loneliness ... How do you describe it?

Loneliness for our son who served in Afghanistan ...

Loneliness for my husband serving in Baghdad, Iraq ...

Our son Donny served with the 501st Army Engineer Company (Geronimo) heavy equipment operations in Afghanistan at Base Salerno in 2004.

I am very proud of him for serving his country, but I was also scared the whole time he was there. I missed him and worried about him being in a combat zone.

When Donny came home from basic training, I noticed a change in him. A good change, he was disciplined, more thoughtful of people and their feelings. But when he came home from combat, I noticed his 1,000-yard stare and wondered what have they done to my son? At times he can be distant and not as trusting as he was before. He had grown into a man ... but then I notice that 1,000-yard stare again, sometimes he just seems to drift off in his mind to another time and place ... and I worry all over again.

Then there is the loneliness I feel for my husband now serving in Iraq at Camp Victory. He is a Lt. Colonel, serving as Liaison Officer with the Combined Joint Special Operations Task Force Arabian Peninsula.

It was a long discussion about him serving in the Army in Iraq. I just couldn't understand his need to serve, until I talked with Denny's brother. He told me how Denny always wanted to play soldier and war games when he was a little boy. How it meant so much for him to graduate from West Point. He helped me to understand Denny's need to go to Iraq, his need to help the people of Iraq find freedom ... so I finally said, "Yes, go if you have to," but I didn't realize, as I spoke, the loneliness I would feel.

This loneliness is eating me from the inside out. I feel like my heart has been taken out of me and stomped on, a part of me is gone while Denny is gone.

I miss my friend, my soul mate. I miss looking across a crowded room and seeing his smile, his amazing smile as he looks at me. I miss having him here to talk about the everyday things. I miss him walking through the door at night, after his long day at work. I miss him holding me, even just holding my hand. And I even miss his snoring or having to sometimes pick up his dirty laundry. Even the dog and cats miss him. They would run to the door when he came home. Sometimes I just hug the dog, Denny's other best friend, and feel a bond with him. The dog looks like I feel … lonely!

We went to seven countries in Europe on R&R. It was a wonderful 14 days. Just being with him again felt so good, but when it came time for him to leave, it was harder this time to let him go. The feelings started all over again, that deep yearning, even deeper than before. Now I knew when I returned home it would be months before he held me again.

I am his second wife. There are eight children between us, so although we may not be the richest of families with money, we sure are rich with children and grandchildren. Our family and friends have helped me get through some of the hard times … the rough times when things go wrong or the house needs fixing. I want to thank all of these friends individually, but I don't want to miss any of the very many friends who have helped me, so I will just say "thank you, to all of you!" I don't know what I would do without your support.

I sometimes go out with these friends, but then I feel guilty about having fun when Denny is not there to share that time with me. Part of me feels I should be at home, another part knows I have to get out once in a while or I'll go crazy being alone.

I have grown since Denny has been away. I can now do all the bills, which I had never done before. I can take care of problems at home, sometimes I need to call on friends to help fix things, but I am not afraid to tackle these task. Denny is proud of me for having the courage to go on while he is away.

One day I was out and got a call on my cell phone. It was from a friend I had not heard from for awhile. Her husband is also in the Army. She had called our home to see how things were going, and asked for Denny. The reply she got was, "Denny is gone." She took this as Denny had been killed in Iraq! She then called my cell phone and in hysterical tears said, "I am so sorry about Denny, I am so sorry Denny died!" I then got hysterical, saying, "No I just talked to him a few hours ago." "No, no", she said, I just asked about him and they said he was gone." Not thinking clearly now, I thought, her husband is also Army, maybe he had heard something.

 The friend I was with now grabbed the phone, "What is going on?" What are you trying to do to Rocky?"

I had died, died inside, thinking my best friend, my soul mate, my Denny had died!

The story got straightened out, but it wasn't until the next day, when I actually heard his voice, that I could feel alive again. Even though I knew the message was all just a mixed up mistake, feelings took over in my mind and body. It was the worst day of my life!

I am usually a very happy person, always fooling around and playing jokes. When I am out somewhere and meet people, they usually ask about Denny. Now I can talk about him for hours, and sometimes I do, but mostly I just say he is okay and I am doing fine. People accept this. What they don't see is how I struggle to put on a happy face, when I am feeling so lonely. They don't see this loneliness or see me crying in our big bed at night … alone! I know I am not the only lonely soldier's wife, but sometimes it feels that way, because if you haven't felt this loneliness, you just can't imagine the empty way your heart feels.

I am a little concerned about changes in him and our relationship. I think there will have to be an adjustment period when he gets home … a year can change people … combat can change a veteran. I just wish everything could go back to what it was like before he left, but I know that's not the way it will be for awhile. I have already noticed changes in him. He does not usually get angry easily, but now, even my not getting one of his phone calls makes him angry. I tried to explain to him that I also have a life. I cannot just sit by the phone waiting for his calls, as important to me as they are. I need to do things for myself, or I would go crazy just waiting for him to come home.

While on R&R when I first saw him, I ran to him and just wanted to hug and kiss him and have him hold me, but after a few seconds he gently pushed me away. I felt so hurt and very angry. Didn't he want me there with him?

And when we first discussed him going to Iraq, he said, "Give me one year and I will hang up my boots." But eight months later he is talking about extending. I don't understand this. Doesn't he also feel the pain of loneliness? My feelings are, come home out of harm's way, you have done your job and I am proud of you, and I know you feel the guys need you, but I also need you.

I have been reading about PTSD, and talking to Marie (the co-author of this book). She understands a lot about PTSD and has been trying to help me understand Denny's way of thinking and comparing it to my way of thinking.

She explained about the anger. He has guys in Iraq that mean a lot to him. When in a combat zone, you bond with the people that are there, they become your family and you worry about them. You are his family back at home, so he also worries about you and when you don't pick up that phone, panic sets in and he wonders, is she okay, did she have an accident, where is she? These are all questions he is asking himself in his way of protecting you from a distance. Her suggestion was to set a time for calls and be there to answer the phone. This would give me time to do things for myself and give him peace of mind when he calls and I am there to answer the phone.

Then she explained about being pushed away. Veterans in a combat zone don't feel they can get too close to anyone. Something might happen to that person and then there is too much pain. So this is brought home to his family – if I love you too much and get too close, I will have to feel that pain if something happens to you. It is very hard to understand that when you are being pushed away. You just have to remember his feelings when this happens.

As of this writing I don't know if Denny will extend or come home. Veterans have a hard time leaving their new family, especially when they are in a combat zone. They feel they need to stay and protect them.

They are trained to be soldiers, not husbands or in some cases wives. This will be the hardest thing to adjust to when they get home. And you have been home doing things your way for a year ... almost going back to that single way of life. The veteran coming home has to adjust to being a husband/wife again and the loved one at home has to adjust also.

I am thankful for Marie's advice, and I will have to read some of the books she has suggested. Thankfully Denny's and my love has not changed. They say, "absence makes the heart grow fonder." I know our love for each other is strong and hopefully that will make things easier.

Loneliness ... how do you describe it?

My heart and mind know no other words but, "it sucks!"

So I will just keep loving him, missing him and singing my song "Come Home Soon"!

Written by Marie Leduc
from an interview with
Rochelle (Rocky) Gum

Remembrance

A romance has just started, but interrupted too,

a boy is called to duty, he will serve the red, white and blue.

His girl back home writes him, and reminds him of the day

the time they had together, before they went away.

For him the time is endless, he is so far from home,

but at least he has tomorrow, and he writes he's not alone.

His time has grown shorter, his time not far away,

10 months he has waited, can he survive the coming days?

A family gets a visit, from a man they do not know,

their son is now a casualty, in a war where others would not go.

His girl is left in mourning, of the days they once knew,

of how they would be wed, and start a life brand new.

As time goes on it's hopeless, fighting sorrow and pain,

of hope and dreams of yesterday, the memory will still remain.

No, it's never over ... yes, life does go on,

we will never forget our brother, that died in Vietnam.

In honor of the women who have suffered the loss
of their loved ones ... to remind them they are not alone
and are one of the many who have sacrificed dreams.

George E. La Bounty

Scars of War

I listened to Dot as she told me a history of family service to our country and how she has felt by having loved ones in four wars, actually five wars, she corrected.

"My great-grandparents were in the Civil War, so being patriotic goes back a long way in my family.

Memorial Day was always a big celebration of parades and putting flags at the graves of veterans. My father was a highly decorated veteran of WWI. He saw a lot of combat, where he was wounded in action. He was always honored at veteran affairs and parades. But at home he didn't pay much attention to family life and often took to drinking his homemade liquor.

I remember when WWII started, the bombing of Pearl Harbor and President Roosevelt saying, 'I declare war!'

My brothers joined, all five of them, and my sister's husband. They were all sent off to war except one who remained stationed in the states."

By now Dot was speaking with concern in her voice, but when she told me the following part of her story, I could hear the pain she has been carrying for over 50 years.

"I was just 15 at the time, my sister became ill with a flu and asked me to help with her children, a two-year-old and a baby of 4 months. I would have the day off from school, but more that that, I really loved those babies.

When she started feeling better, she asked if I would stay another day so she could go to church that evening. While at church, she met a Russian gentleman. They talked for awhile about the war and what was happening. When she arrived home that evening, I thought she seemed more at peace as she spoke of her conversation with the Russian gentleman. But, upon awakening the next morning, she was upset. She said she had a dream, but maybe it was only because of speaking with the gentleman the night before.

Her dream was about her husband and the words he spoke in the dream was upsetting her … As she told me, those words also upset me. I tried to put them out of my mind and started breakfast. It was about 8:00, we had just sat down to eat when there was a knock on the door. A young kid delivering a Western Union telegram … my sister's husband had been killed in action."

As Dot spoke, I could see the tears in her eyes and her voice started to shake, but she went on.

"My sister became hysterical, so the burden of telling his and our family was left up to me … not an easy task for a 15-year-old. I know I got the message to everyone, but after that I don't remember anything that happened for about 3 days.

By now I had my own feelings about war. I missed my brothers and worried about them, always questioning in my mind, if they would come home. Being in a patriotic family, I kept my feelings to myself. I just kept thinking, they are fighting for our country, our rights and our freedom.

When the war was over all of my brothers came home and life went on. One of my brothers decided to make the Army his career. The way he put it was, 'I was washing windows for the officers one day, thinking, someday I'm going to be on the inside watching someone else do these windows.'

Then in 1953 when the war in Korea started, again he went off to war. When our dad passed away, my brother was deep in a combat zone and was not notified about the death for quite some time, which was a very upsetting situation for him. "When he came home he didn't talk much about his time in combat. He only told us the funny stories about himself and the guys."

Time went on for Dot and again she put war out of her mind, but ten years later, her brother was back at war, this time in Vietnam, doing not one, but two tours. "When he came home this time he only spoke of one incident. It was Christmas Eve and he was an officer by now. He and a friend were in a hotel in Saigon when the hotel was bombed. He was flung up against the wall by a window and got tangled in the curtains, which caused his injury. When things cleared up a bit, he saw his buddy on the floor … another casualty of war."

When he left the Army he was a Lt. Colonel and probably did watch someone else wash those windows, but Dot wonders if it was all worth it.

I asked Dot for her brother's address, I would have liked to talk with him. Her reply was, "It's too late now, he suffers with Alzheimer's disease … all he talks about now is the war, things he has kept inside for so long just seem to pour out, but in no order. He is now feeling the traumatic emotions of war."

I think Dot telling me her story of her loved ones in combat and her receiving the telegram with her sister shows the trauma she has felt all these years.

Her husband is also a veteran, he didn't serve in combat, but Dot will tell you, "While he was away, it was the loneliest, most awful time of my life."

The effects of serving one's country, especially in time of war, are felt by so many veterans and loved ones … leaving scars upon all who are affected.

Written by Marie Leduc

From an interview with Dot Liken

Michael's reflection looks upon his mother as she touches his name on "The Wall".

A Gold Star Mother's Thoughts

There it stands ... that long black marble Wall ...

So many names ... who answered the call.

They believed ... and only did what they were told ...

And now their names are on that Wall ... so very cold.

But the love in our hearts ... still stays warm ...

Their faces and memories of them ... in our arms.

They will always be a part of our lives ...

But we have to move on ... and learn to survive.

Thanks to the veterans ... who gave their all ...

We honor them ... when we come to the Wall.

We don't need to grieve ... but we need to stand tall ...

And be proud of everyone ... who gave their all.

Dorothy Schafernocker

Michael

It's early morning, still dark outside. Mike is leaving for basic training in the Navy. I am his mother standing on the front porch watching him walk off in the darkness … tears in my eyes, thinking back to his days of growing up. I have done what I could … taught him right from wrong, to help others when they needed help … to just follow the golden rule. But I was also thinking, God you gave him to me and I did what I could, now I am giving him back to you to watch over him …Please help him to remember all I have taught him!

Basic training and all his other training went well. Mike came home on leave … time that was very special … because …

"Why … Why … Why … Why did Mike have to die, Lord?" He was only 20 years and two months old … to the day!

"Lord, what have I said or done? I tried to be a good mother … I know I have made mistakes in my life and I am still making them, but why did you have to take Mike … my son? He was such a good kid, never gave us any problems. Why Lord? Where did I go wrong? Why didn't I die? I have lived a good life, long in many respects, but Mike had his whole life before him!"

My life had been good … till this happened! Yes, I have had my ups and downs, good days and bad, but nothing has ever hurt me like losing my son. I have lost other loved ones in my life, but my son Mike? "It isn't fair, Lord! Why am I being punished?"

I will never forget the day … yes that day! Jack and I were just sitting down for lunch, the door bell rang. I went to the door, I saw the man standing there with his wife, he was dressed in his Navy blues … and before he could even say a word, I screamed and could feel myself falling to the floor. The Navy Chaplin opened the screen door to try to catch me, but before he could, my husband was there to hold me … and hold me … and hold me!

I just knew before the Chaplin could even say a word, I knew something had happened to Mike. I felt so empty, like someone had reached inside and pulled everything out … like a part of me had died too!

Those words and pleas have gone over and over in my mind, at least what seemed to be what was left of my mind. I felt I could still feel his movement in my body before he was born, it was so very special, but I still couldn't seem to get away from asking why … nothing seemed to make sense to me.

We were told by the Navy that Mike, with his pilot Dick Reardon, and his co-pilot Hal Castle, were actually buried in Cambodia. Yes, I know the U.S. government was not talking about having anyone in Cambodia, but that's where he and his crew were.

Ten months later, the very weekend of Mike's 21st birthday, they sent us a casket. It was sealed and we were not allowed to open it. We were told it contained a small bag of bones. We accepted the casket and Mike was buried in Arlington, Texas.

I never knew I had that many tears inside of me … I found myself crying at all times of the day and night. I felt so hopeless, so empty! It was a feeling that wouldn't go away for a very long time. Someone said, "The good die young and the young die good." I guess there is more truth than poetry in that statement.

Though it has taken a long time to try to get back to living, and it seems even a longer time to make sense of why it happened, the good Lord did have a plan for my life and that of Mike's.

I can't remember exactly when the following happened, but I honestly believe it was the answer to my whys … and it helped to give me my life back … my family back. I have another son, Ronnie, who I am sure felt so lonely when he found out his brother was never coming home, and my husband Jack, Mike's dad … he must have suffered, it is also his son who died. And they had lost me too! But then God spoke to me.

Jack and I were sound asleep, it was early in the morning and I heard a deep man's voice say, "Dorothy." It startled me from my sleep. I thought someone was in our home … and then just that quick I heard the voice again, "Dorothy … Michael did what he had to do on this earth, I have other plans for him … but I'm not done with you!"

By that time I was sitting straight up in bed, expecting to see a man at the foot of my bed … but no one was there! My movement woke Jack, asking what was wrong … I said nothing was really wrong and tried to explain what had just happened. He said, "you're just dreaming, go back to sleep, it was just a bad dream!" But was it just a dream? … I don't believe it was, those words were burned into my heart, and even though it did take time, those words did come true.

Jack divorced me after 30 years of marriage … so now I was on my own … I had to do something with my life.

I was given the job of driving one of the "Moving Walls," a half size replica of the Vietnam Memorial in Washington, D.C. It travels all over the United States … taking

"The Wall" of 58,000+ names of those who died in Vietnam, to those who cannot get to Washington, D.C. It brings healing to many veterans, mothers, fathers, brothers, and sisters, friends, and to anyone who knows a "Name On The Wall"!

I drove September thru November 1989 and April thru November 1990 ... all over the U.S.A. ... just me and those 58,000+ guys on "The Wall" looking after me ... especially Mike!

It was a big step in my healing ... talking to vets who had been in country ... especially when they found out my son's name was on that "Wall." It made them realize that I did know why they were also hurting. Although I had not been in country with them, I had also lost a part of my life to Vietnam ... just as they had lost their brothers, I had lost my son, not exactly the same, but the hurt, the loss, the feelings are the same. As I walked with them along "The Wall" talking, crying, remembering ... we healed, hugged, and felt a small sense of peace ... I needed them ... just as much as they needed a mother's touch!

I also got in touch with the Navy Seawolves ... Mike's squadron in Vietnam. I have been to all of their reunions I have known about ... these guys are truly wonderful and have treated me like a mom for sure ... nicknaming me "Momma." I bring all the pictures, poems and other things I have of Mike's or things that have been given to me ... and we all talk about Mike or Vietnam ... but now as years pass and I have so many sons (and daughters too) we mostly talk about the things going on in our lives today. What a wonderful healing for me!

No it isn't me, it's the good Lord ... see, He did keep His word to me ... He did have plans for our lives. We just have to "let go ... and let God!"

Mike wrote all kinds of poetry and I find that repeating what he wrote is a wonderful tool in healing! Yes ... Good can come from death!

"Momma"
Dorothy Schafernocker

Look, God

Look, God, I have never spoken to you,
But now I want to say, "How do you do."
You see, God, they told me you didn't exist.
And like a fool, I believed all this.

Last night from a shell hole, I saw your sky.
I figured right then, they had told me a lie.
Had I taken time to see the things you made,
I'd have known they weren't calling a spade a spade.

I wonder, God, if you'd shake my hand,
Somehow, I feel you will understand.
Funny ... I had to come to this hellish place ...
Before I had to see your face.

Well, I guess there isn't much more to say,
But I'm glad, God, that I met you today!
I guess the zero hour will soon be here,
But I am not afraid since I know you're near!

The signal ... well, God, I'll have to go.
I like you lots and want you to know.
Look now ... this will be a horrible fight...
Why who knows ... I may come to your house tonight!

Though I wasn't friendly to you before ...
I wonder, God, if you'd wait by your door.
Look ... I'm crying ... me shedding tears!
I wish I'd have known you these many years.

Well, God, I'll have to go now ... goodbye ...
Strange, since I have met you, I'm not afraid to die.
Shade of laughter, shades of love,
Circling all of us, with arms of love.
Don't cry, "Momma," I love you still
I always have and I always will!
When you cross the big divide...
I promise ... I'll be the first one by your side!

Michael Schafernocker
Navy Seawolf
Killed In Action 04-28-69

In the Cage

It is July in Waterbury, Connecticut … people are gathering at Library Park … it is the weekend of the 40-hour Prisoner of War/Missing in Action (POW-MIA) vigil.

The first hour begins, it is always special because it honors all wars. Speakers talk about the newest information on the POW-MIA situation. It is an emotional hour … but each hour is emotional as a POW enters the cage and another is welcomed home.

It is now the 39th hour … Doris walks from behind the curtain, dressed in black pajamas … she pins the red ribbon with her brother's name on the POW-MIA flag, salutes, walks over to the cage … it is lifted, the prisoner is released … Doris welcomes him home … how hard it must be, wishing in her heart this was Andre coming home … instead she must walk beneath the cage and let it be lowered … to be imprisoned in his place … as these visions and thoughts, ever present, are more vivid for her hour … in the cage!

I stand here
with chains on my hands and feet.
"Andre,
are you chained too … have you been beat?
Like me,
do you stand in a cage of bamboo?
I plead,
please tell me … where are you?

33 years
I'm waiting … so much time gone by,
with questions,
so many questions … all asking why.
Always in my mind
I see your eyes … through tears, your face.
How,
I ask … could you disappear without a trace?

Brother of mine,

wish I could send you a card ... today,

Happy Birthday!

Two small boys in big jeans ... just walkin' away,

so cute

just walkin' ... fishing rods in hand ...

Oh, memories,

my throat tightens ... how much more can I stand?

Friends

when you were little boys ... you and Paul.

Today,

he has 2 sons ... your name is on "The Wall!"

My husband

David ... also faithful to you all these years,

my mentor

he's been here with me ... through all the tears.

I stand tall

as the cage is lifted ... I look up not down ...

see the flag,

so beautiful ... as it flies over your hometown.

My tears fall,

my rosary is pressed in my hand ... and I pray,

Andre,

so many here remember you ... please, come home someday!"

The 40th hour has arrived ... many have gathered to welcome Doris home, many with thoughts of ... if only this was real ... Andre, with other MIA's standing among their brothers, family and friends who have been waiting for years to say, "Welcome home!"

Marie Leduc

Doris Maitland standing in the cage representing her brother, Andre Guillet, who is still Missing In Action from the Vietnam War.

Still Hopes He Will Come Marching Home To Us

My brother served in Vietnam from April 1965 to May 1966 for a total of eleven months. He was located at Nakhom Phanom Air Base in Thailand. He was assigned to the 1st Air Commando Wing and TDY to 606 Air Command Squadron. His duty was as a Combat Controller flying back seat in an O1E working as a forward air controller directing air strikes on the Ho Chi Minh Trail. He was awarded a Purple Heart and a Distinguished Flying Cross and held the rank of Airman Second Class.

This is my story:

There are 58,000 names inscribed on the Vietnam Wall in Washington, DC. Each name has a story to tell. Some names are followed by a star. Their story has an ending. Some names are followed by a cross. Their story has no closure, they are the POW/MIA. On wall 7 east, line 81 is inscribed the name SMSgt Andre R. Guillet. He is my brother and we have waited for him to come home since 1966.

Andre was born in Waterbury, CT on Dec. 17, 1943. Our family lived on East Liberty Street on the second floor of a three family house. My mom and Andre arrived home on Christmas day – a special gift to his Dad and sisters aged 6 and 11. As a young baby he howled through the night and was cranky and very special. He was adored by his family. It wasn't long before he was climbing and jumping. I realized how special he was when at the age of 10 months he became suspended by his diaper hanging on the knob of the top pantry cupboard.

At age 18 months he managed to topple a step stool and suffered a 3-inch cut above his left eyebrow. At age five he jumped down a flight of cement steps and split his upper lip. Instead of coming home to be tended to he stayed outdoors and played until it was too late to have a doctor stitch it up.

He was tiny and tough and fearless. Not an outstanding scholar. He preferred to fish, ride his bike and hunt down turtles, frogs and toads. One of his best friends was his dog Nipper, a small terrier mutt who hopped about on only three useful legs.

When Andre was seven our family moved to a new home and he cultivated a new set of friends. Many of them are still in touch with our family. One friend, Paul Parkosewich, has been the moving force in keeping Andre's case open. He is tireless in tracking down leads on Andre's situation.

In 1961, Andre graduated from Sacred Heart High School. He joined the Y.M.C.A. and trained in judo competition and achieved the degree of brown belt. He attended the University of CT and was employed by the Waterbury Park Department. He was a member of St. Mary Magdalene Church.

His restlessness at a time when our government was becoming involved in the S.E. Asian Conflict influenced his decision to join the Air Force. He completed basic training at Lackland Air Force Base in Texas and Radio Operator training at Kessler Air Force Base in Mississippi. He applied for and was accepted into the Air Commandos, the special forces of the Air Force. When I asked him why he chose that group he said it was the only outfit where you didn't have to shine your own shoes. He completed the Combat Control Team Training at Eglin Air Force Base in FL. He was awarded a special citation for developing the zone parachute drop concept. His technical skill was as a radio communications expert and at last a parachute jumper. What he loved most was the physical aspects of training.

He excelled in the jungle and desert survival school. He qualified in small arms and was an expert in hand-to-hand combat. During a parachute jumping exercise in 1965, he jumped out of a plane at 3,000 feet. When his chute failed he threw out his emergency chute. That chute only developed partially. As a result he landed on a concrete runway suffering a minor break in his back, ruined boots and extremely sore feet. After a week in the hospital he returned to Waterbury for R&R. He immediately began a program of personal training. He told me he wanted to be ready to jump by the end of the month so he wouldn't lose his hazard pay. He didn't lose it.

Andre was eager to go to Vietnam. He told us the Communists had to be defeated so his five young nephews would never have to go to war. He spent his last Christmas with the family. There was an unspoken fear that cooled our Christmas joy but Andre enjoyed his leave. He was soon on his way to S.E. Asia. We received several letters … Hawaii was wonderful … He invented a new sport called aqua surfing. The Air Force treated him to champagne and filet mignon. Next stop Thailand. He couldn't tell us what he was doing but he'd never seen a more beautiful, dangerous country.

His group did a parachute demo for the locals. Andre fell through the roof on a Buddhist temple and was decorated by the resident monk. His last letter was dated May 14, 1966. He had been on a Civic Action Project between reconnaissance flights. I quote from his letter, "This civic project consisted of giving medical aid, helping to build roads, give parachute demos and anything else that will make them think we were good guys. These people are polite and friendly. I would help them more if I could."

On May 18, 1966, two men in Air Force uniforms came to my parent's home to tell us Andre and his pilot were missing in action. They could not have imagined the anguish and sorrow their message brought. Our questions were endless and the men answered what they could. Where was he lost? – North Vietnam. What was he doing? – Flying backseater in a two man plane. His pilot is also missing. How long must we wait for news? – The government is doing everything possible to find them. So we prepared to wait. A week, a month, thirty-five years. At first we were consoled by family and friends but some became strangely silent about Andre's loss. My life was busy raising four young boys and teaching full time. But not a day went by when this terror would suddenly overcome me. My co-workers and friends never knew. I could not speak about it lest I lose my composure. It was too raw, too overwhelming to think about.

The government would send information periodically. They said that they were doing everything possible. We were advised not to speak about the case with anyone but family for fear of endangering the lives of the missing. We followed orders, this was the U.S.A., we could trust our government. But skepticism crept in. A phone call from the father of Andre's pilot informed us that the plane was shot down over Laos, not North Vietnam. Laos was a neutral country … U.S. forces were not supposed to be there.

Christmas 1966 … memories of last year's celebration flooded our eyes. Tears clouded the holiday celebration. But there were also moments of laughter when we recalled Andre's sense of humor and the playfulness he exhibited with his nephews. The backyard camping trip with four little guys – teaching them to eat ants, sleep in the woods, hunting for porcupine, showing them how to frighten adults by letting a daddy long leg spider hang out of the side of their mouth.

Years went by with memorial masses celebrated on Andre's birthday.

During the war Andre's job was to fly from Nakhom Phanom airbase in Thailand over the Ho Chi Minh trail in Laos. On these missions he flew backseater and directed air strikes along enemy lines. It was on one of these missions that the O1E plane was shot down. He and his pilot Capt. Lee Harley have not returned. We received much support from family groups and veterans groups and veterans organizations. They are dedicated to returning POW/MIA from all wars. We have also been enriched by the friends and family members of the missing. We are brought together by our common pain. We have forged new friendships with Andre's military friends. We are associate members of the Air Commandos Association and the Combat Controllers Association.

The empty spaces in Andre's life have been filled with their recollections of their time with him. His friends have become our friends. Andre's name is inscribed on several monuments. We are grateful for the honor but I am reminded of the words of Tom Cleary, the brother of an MIA, when he said, "There are no funerals for the missing."

The annual scrub sheet on Andre's case sent by the DOD/POW/MIA in 2003 indicated a possibility that the crash site has been found with the help of three former North Vietnamese soldiers. This was the most positive news we have received to date. At a September 2004 government briefing held in Farmington, CT I learned that the case was slated for excavation in two to three years. Closure is near and yet the tugging voice of my heart still hopes that he will come marching home to us.

Doris Maitland

Learning to Accept You ...
When Your Vet has PTSD

There are 5 stages of the grief process ...*

Denial ...

    Anger ...

      Bargaining ...

        Depression ...

          Acceptance ...

Let's go through these stages, comparing them to living with a veteran who has Post Traumatic Stress Disorder and learning to live with you.

Did you know your vet before he went to war? Were you married while he was in country? This could make a difference in your relationship.

Did he come home with a different personality? Did you realize just a few days before he was fighting a war ... watching others die, getting wounded and wondering who would be next, as he left his brothers behind. Now he is back in "the world" wondering where he is, what he is doing here and don't these people know there is a war going on?

No, we didn't realize that, we simply thought, you're home now, war is behind you, so let's just go back to "normal," back to what we had before. We wanted them to forget it all happened. That may have been a long time ago, but are you still living with his memories?

It may be a new relationship. He doesn't mention war or his experiences while in country. He may not even tell you he is a veteran. He is a great guy, but you notice his alienation, anxiety or rage. How do you react to these situations?

He could be a veteran who has realized something is wrong, has heard of PTSD and sought counseling. He may understand isolation, depression or survival guilt, but his pain never really goes away. He may continue to have flashbacks and nightmares. Common everyday experiences such as smells, sounds and sights can easily trigger memories. Do you know these triggers?

Our situations may all be different, but it all comes back to the same question ... how do we live with our vet now ... so many years after the war?

133

Let's go back to the grief process ...

Denial ... We as the loved ones of veterans can deny his PTSD or we can learn all about it. Your veteran may not agree, but for your own sake, you need to know the symptoms and how they affect your vet, so you can stop blaming yourself for his emotions and actions.

A psychologist describes PTSD as a normal reaction to an abnormal amount of trauma or as one counselor put it in more understandable terms, "take the worst traumatic time in your life and think how it would be to live it 24 hours a day for 365 or more days."

We have to learn everything about PTSD. We have to dig deep to learn about his experiences. He may not talk about his time at war or won't admit he has PTSD. "How am I supposed to learn the answers" question many loved ones.

He is not your only source of information.

There are many books about PTSD ... read a few! Two of my favorites for wives and loved ones are *Recovering From The War* by Patience Mason and *Vietnam Wives* by Aphrodite Matsakis.

Go on the internet, type in Post Traumatic Stress Disorder. You will find hundreds of web sites and links.

Go to your closest Vet Center, Vets Outreach Center or VA. They all have free counseling. Some have wives groups, where you can talk freely with others who live with PTSD in their daily lives.

Find a book about his unit when he was at war. These authors tell you what it was really like, because in their own way they want you to understand the traumas of war.

Anger ... Are you angry with his PTSD? Do you fight back, causing an argument, so either you or he can walk out?

We don't have to walk on eggshells just because he has PTSD. We can learn to be caring and loving, not only to him, but also to ourselves.

If his PTSD starts to surface, ask him if he needs help or wants to talk? At first this may make him angry, but as time goes by he will see you care and may respond.

In the meantime use your anger constructively ... go for a walk, do a craft, anger is a great time to do a cleaning project. Do something for yourself.

Remember the PTSD is his, if you get angry, you are then taking on your own emotion. It is important you think about what is making you angry. "A problem is a problem until it is solved" (Hugh Prather ... *I Touch The Earth The Earth Touches Me*). Figure out why you are angry, find a solution ... if you aren't happy, how are those around you supposed to be happy?

Bargaining ... Do you say, "Why me?" Do you blame God or a Higher Power? "Why did you put me in this situation?" "It's not fair to have to live like this!"

Then why are you living in this situation? Most likely because you love your vet ... You – no one else chose to live with him. "But, he wasn't like this when I made that choice" many say. You still have a choice! If you are in an abusive situation, think carefully, maybe you need to leave for your own safety. If the situation is not abusive, again think carefully ... think of the good times, the loving times and have fun with those times.

Don't blame anyone else. Question yourself to find the answers. Make choices that are right for you.

Depression ... Do you sometimes feel sad, lonely or worthless? You think maybe it's just not worth living another day. Do you take on these feelings when his PTSD is surfacing?

STOP!

Remember it is his PTSD not yours. Don't let him bring you down with his moods.

Find ways to pick yourself up. Find your interest ... then pursue them. Find a friend ... go visit them. Find a Higher Power and talk to Him.

I'm not saying you should constantly be away from your vet, but make some time for you, time to do the things you like. You do not have to take care of everyone, but you do have to take care of you.

Acceptance ... When you stop denying his PTSD you can accept his moods better, because you will know they are his feelings.

Accept your anger, knowing it is your emotion and only you can learn to control it in constructive ways.

Bargaining doesn't give you choices, it gives you excuses. Accept your choices.

Do not accept depression. Find yourself so you can accept happiness in your life.

A very wise person told me to "Live for the moment!" As I began to protest his statement, arguing it's too hard to live for the moment, he interrupted me, "I didn't say it would be easy." I then remembered a lesson he had taught me that started, "It's not easy ... it's necessary!"

No it is not easy to go through the grief process, but it is necessary in learning to accept you. Maybe then you can change the grief process to the serenity process!

GRIEF PROCESS		**SERENITY PROCESS**
Denial	can change to	Learning
Anger	to	Caring
Bargaining	to	Choices
Depression	to	Happiness
Acceptance	and you will	Accept You!

The Grief Process was originally written by Elizabeth Kubler-Ross

The Serenity Process is written by Marie Leduc

How Certain Dates Affect Veterans with Post Traumatic Stress Disorder

For some veterans any holiday or anniversary date may bring their stress to a very high level. An anniversary date to a veteran is a date on which something in combat may have happened, such as a major battle, a buddy getting killed, an ambush, etc. The holidays are the ones people celebrate throughout the year, such as birthdays, Christmas, Thanksgiving, Memorial Day, Veterans Day, etc.

If you look at the numbers of those wounded during holidays, you will see the numbers go up. The reason may be, the veteran, just for a moment, may have been thinking of home and family and may have lost their concentration of what was going on around him/her.

When veterans come home these dates have a lasting effect on them, also affecting their family as well. I asked veterans how these anniversary dates and the holidays affect them. Maybe some of the answers will help you understand the feelings your veteran has during this time of the year.

"Thanksgiving is a more important holiday. It is a time to bring the family together without all the hype of Christmas. It's not as pressured or commercialized."

"It can be summed up in two words … holidays suck!"

"It can be physiological, smells of things cooking … bodies burning. Sounds, kids noises … kids in a combat zone. It is also contradictory, there was a Christmas tree in Nam, I wanted to smash it. Peace on earth … we were blowing people away. Then the survivor guilt gets in there, I'm still alive, yet we were still killing or being killed. We got drunk to bury the feelings and a lot of us do the same today."

Another said, "I believe veterans lose the meaning because during holidays the fear of getting close to family causes a red flag to go up, so they shy away."

This veteran thinks, "I didn't lose the holidays in Nam, I believe I lost the meaning, the spirituality or faith connected, but not only for holidays, but all the days the rest of my life."

A couple of veterans came up with this answer, "It's no big deal, in Nam it was just another day, now years later … still no big deal, just another day."

One veteran related this: "Most of my problems associated with the holidays are related to the idea that I always expect someone else, like my wife, to make the time enjoyable for all. I withhold my participation, but react with anger if things go wrong. I don't want to do anything … I just want to be left alone, withdraw into my own safe little world of nothingness, where nothing can make me happy, but again, nothing can harm me either. It can be an extremely difficult task for a wife or family member to have much effect on what their vet chooses to do with their mood swings. Their emotions are their own and if they choose to keep them locked up, it can be difficult to find the right key – especially since it's apparent that the vet has swallowed the key and keeps it safely inside him."

This vet said, "I believe holidays are an attitude, a time when your imagination should pull away from reality, if only for a short time, to find the joy, fun, giving, love and peace. Speaking as a vet, I think finding these emotions have been difficult. War can deal you a harsh dose of reality, far from the above mentioned emotions. When we start remembering, we don't reflect and act on the first part of our lives. When this process is put into motion, war memories are overwhelmingly stronger and we find that we truly have been transformed by this experience."

"In coming home, I felt like I never did, that I lost my country. I believe many of the wives and families felt they had lost us, that maybe we were just a dream left behind … there physically, but non-existent of the person who left."

With tears in his eyes, this vet spoke of his children. "I am divorced, the children are mostly with their mom. But when holidays are here, especially Father's Day, I want to see my children, but their mom only lets me see them for a short time, if at all. She takes them to visit her relatives, this makes me feel very hurt and angry, the lack of respect for me being their father. I should have more time with my children, especially on Father's Day … I am their dad, this should be my day!"

Their anniversary dates should be known by the family – that is if the veteran tells them about those dates. Again the sights, sounds, and smells can trigger a reaction, causing flashbacks, numbing out, time spent alone just thinking of what happened during that time period. This is a time when alcohol or drugs may take over in the vet's life. This is a time when a lot of families really walk on eggshells. Until the time has passed or the veteran has sought help, there is not much a family can do for the vet, but they can still go on with their own lives. It can be very difficult for the family to do this, knowing their loved one is suffering. They can not let the vet drag them down with his/her feelings. This is when the family has to really be their own person and do things to make themselves happy and worthwhile. Talk with your vet, ask if there is anything you can do to help him/her. This may initiate an argument from the veteran, but at least you know you have offered help … and so does your vet!

Marie Leduc

"Happy Veterans Day"
Writing from Observation

Today is Veteran's Day and we're going to the Veterans Hospital to see
their dad. The boys and I went to the parade in town. We had a wonderful
time, the streets were full of marching bands, bright colored balloons and
a thundering cheering crowd. Still full from all the excitement, the boys
chattered all the way to the hospital. They asked a million questions, one
of which was "Why are there only a few Vietnam veterans in the parade?" I tried as hard as I could to explain it, but all I could come up with
was that most Nam vets don't like crowds. How can you explain the
devastating damages of war to the wide-eyed innocents who think of
their dad as a hero?

I park the car and we begin the hike up the steep hill to the hospital. The closer to the
building we get, the fiercer the wind seems. It's so bitterly cold up here! A strong damp
wind circles our legs as we draw nearer to the front door. It seems so bleak up on the hill.
I'm not sure if it's the cold November day or the overall mood that seems to hang over
this place like a dark cloud of sadness.

As we approach the front of the building, we see a small group of men hanging around
the entrance. There aren't many guys left here on weekends, just a few with no place to
go and no way to get there. There's old Joe, sitting in a wheelchair with one leg missing
just above the knee and the other covered with bandages. He is a jolly soul, always
smiling, happy for the company of anyone who will listen to his tales of the "good old
days." The days of "his" war, World War II, he says, "That was a real war!"

Nearby stands a few younger men, like sentries at their post. So solemn, so vigilant, they
watch every movement and jump at every noise.

Gunner, a friend of dad's, stands with his back to the cold cement wall. He recognizes us
and with a small quick smile says, "Hi!" Gunner stands about six feet tall, with long
brown hair streaked with an overabundance of premature gray, pulled back in a neat
ponytail. A full beard and mustache cover his sullen features like a mask. He looks too
old for a young man of only forty-six. Despite the overcast of the gloomy November sky,
he still wears mirrored sunglasses. If memory serves me right, he has beautiful blue eyes,
but in all the years we've known him, Gunner has seldom taken off his sunglasses. This is
true of a lot of Nam vets.

"What are they hiding from?" some people ask. Do they really want to know? Have they ever looked into those cloaked eyes or taken the time to see the pain of their open wounds that still ache in the pit of their souls? So many stand in silence, crying to be heard. Many years have passed, yet if you look deep enough, you can still see the terrified little boys of yesterday.

My husband comes through the double doors and meets us with eager anticipation. It's only been a few days since we've seen him, but to look at him, you would think it had been months. He gently kisses my cheek and hugs the boys as we say goodbye to the few who will remain.

A nurse passes in her crisp white uniform. She smiles cheerfully at our forgotten heroes and says, "Happy Veteran's Day, boys." The guys glance at each other in amazement and then in what seems like a choreographed movement they look toward the ground. After an obedient chorus of "Thank you" each man retreats back into his own silence.

As we head toward the car, I can hear one of the vets ask soulfully, "How can Veteran's Day be happy?"

Adele Lavigne

The Moving Wall

I stood at a distance …

Looking at the long black line, knowing there is a center … the beginning, the apex of the wall. Extending to the right, names … thousands of names. I look to the left and follow the black line until I reach the center again … the end. Names – over 58,000 on the moving wall.

I feel the wall move … my wall … the wall within!

I step a little closer …

I know the names are there, but I am still too far away to see them.

I feel the wall move again … my wall … maybe just a crack!

I feel the fear, but I must get closer, as the names call out to me. I see faces in the jungle … if I get close enough … will I see the faces in the wall?

I feel the wall … moving inside myself!

Someone places his hand on my shoulder. I can't look at him, just feel he is there with me … as I step slowly closer … then closer … until finally I can see the names, the faces … hear them talking …

Tears are rolling down my cheeks, washing away part of my wall … years of building … washed away with tears for my brothers who died in a foreign land. Side by side we fought, as now I walk side by side of the 58,000 ... looking for his name … best friends, for a time in Nam.

I stand there frozen in time …

25 years ago! Memories, pain, anger … tears flooding out of my eyes. The hand that was on my shoulder is now embracing me. I can hardly stand … I am shaking so, breaking apart pieces of the wall … my wall … the wall within.

How long have I stood here … today? … 25 years? …

Seems like only yesterday I was in Nam … But, maybe today I saw "The World" again for the first time!

I saw his face within the wall … felt him there with me … felt his embrace, as the pieces of the wall came tumbling down …

I felt the moving wall … my wall … the wall within!

Marie Leduc

The "Moving Wall" is a scale model of the Vietnam Veterans Memorial "Wall" in Washington, D.C. It is moved around the country, so those who cannot get to Washington, D.C. can still feel the effects of the 58,000+ names on black granite.

Veterans also build a wall around themselves when they have witnessed combat, and come home with PTSD … the wall within!

Sometimes going to "The Wall" helps a veteran to heal from the emotions brought back from the war.

How Post Traumatic Stress Disorder Affects the Children of Combat Veterans

Symptoms of Post Traumatic Stress Disorder can have an effect on the way in which a combat veteran relates to others. Children of these veterans may develop low self esteem, hyperactivity, poor reality testing or aggressive behavior.

These children could exhibit one of three patterns, the most destructive being the over-identified child. This child can experience emotions similar to a veteran with PTSD. The child is often the veteran's closest companion and is at risk of "reliving" the veteran's trauma, experiencing his/her flashbacks or sharing their nightmares. They fail to develop their own friendships because their lives revolve around the veteran. In school they may have trouble concentrating because of their concern for their parent's well being.

Another pattern is becoming "rescuers." The child may take on the parent's role and responsibilities. They may feel guilty about trouble at home and blame themselves. They feel responsible for keeping the veteran happy, making sure nothing goes wrong.

The third pattern centers on children who are emotionally uninvolved in family life. These children may know about the veteran's combat experiences and need for support, but usually receive little emotional support from the veteran. Trying to gain recognition, they may do well academically, but their emotional and social constriction might cause depression and anxiety, later causing problems during adulthood with intimate relationships.

Some families may have problems with communication and problem solving. There may also be problems with substance abuse or violence. Other families may have an extremely close relationship and may be overprotective or controlling.

Silence can be a message as traumatic as words. Silence communicates rules and messages to children. It may be taken in two ways. First, the child may work hard to avoid doing anything to cause the symptoms of PTSD in their parent. Second, the veteran's behavior may inhibit discussion about sensitive issues. A combat veteran may react with extreme anxiety, outbursts of rage, or flashbacks. Children quickly learn to avoid talking about events or emotions they believe may cause such behavior. Children who live with veterans with PTSD may be continually exposed to this behavior. The child may feel responsible for the parent's distress and feel if they could be good enough their parent would not be so angry or sad.

Children seek out the veteran's acceptance and recognition. They may identify with the veteran's experience and feel what he feels. Veterans may be unpredictable and explosive during intrusions, unable or unwilling to explain what is happening to them. The veteran may feel guilty and isolate themselves or feel emotionally numb and be unable to connect with the child. The children may have the same feelings and behaviors.

A child may watch their parent go into a restaurant and sit in the far corner with his/her back against the wall, a place where he/she cannot be surprised or no one could ambush him/her. The child could learn to have similar feelings on the playground, thinking there are dangers in the world for which he or she must be on guard.

Combat veterans with Post Traumatic Stress Disorder may tend to reenact their trauma. Children may find themselves thinking, feeling and believing they too have been traumatized. Children may learn the message of distrust. This message may be intentional from his/her veteran parent, but often involves unconscious acting out. When children experience this they are being secondarily traumatized.

Not all children with parents that are combat veterans with PTSD have problems. Some children have positive responses from their parent.

When writing this book, I asked a number of children of combat veterans to write their story of how their parent's PTSD affected them. Some children said they wanted to write something, but did not know how to express what they feel. Some were afraid they may upset the veteran if they told the truth about how they felt. And others said they felt no problems from living with a parent with Post Traumatic Stress Disorder.

Marie Leduc

He Said He Had No Friends

Dear Mom and Dad,

*The war is done; my task is through; but, Mom, there's something I must ask of you.
I have a friend; Oh, such a friend! Homeless, you see; and so I would like to bring him
home with me.*

Dear Son,

We don't mind if someone comes home with you; perhaps, he could stay a week or two.

Dear Mom,

There's something you must know; now please don't be alarmed.

My friend was in a battle recently, where he was hurt and lost an arm.

Dear Son,

*Don't be alarmed to bring him home with you; perhaps he could stay and visit a
day or two.*

Dear Mom,

*But, Mother, he's not just a friend; he's like a brother, too, that's why I want him with us
and like a son to you. Before you give me your answer, Mom, I really don't care to beg;
but, my friend fought in a battle in which he lost a leg.*

Dear Son,

It hurts to say my answer must be no. For Dad and I have no time for a boy crippled so.

*So months went by; a letter came. It said their boy had died and when they read the cause
of death it was suicide.*

Days later when the casket came ...

Draped in our country's flag,

They saw their son lying there,

Without an arm or leg!

Author Unknown

Treatment

Cognitive Behavior Therapy

Along with behavior therapies certain medications are helpful for the treatment of PTSD. Cognitive behavior therapy: The therapist's goal is to help the veteran change their irrational beliefs, such as self-blame, criminal assault, anxiety, and accidents. The behavior consists of stress management using techniques such as slow abdominal breathing, avoid hyperventilation, positive thinking, and self-talk to replace negative thoughts.

Stress Management Techniques

Learn relaxation techniques to reduce the anxiety. The therapist teaches the techniques to reduce the stress caused by the trauma. Using breathing techniques and abdominal breathing along with positive thoughts, including positive affirmations on a daily basis can help. Learn and use relaxation technologies, such as progressive relaxation, scanning relaxation, deep muscle relaxation, count down relaxation, imagery training, mental simulation and the zero content consciousness drill. Biofeedback also helps to relax one's mind and body.

Desensitization Therapy

Learn effective ways to relax and control the thoughts of the traumatic event, including meditation to diminish the thoughts of the event. Repeatedly expose yourself to the source of the anxiety. In my case I would force myself to watch fireworks on TV. I then could listen to the sounds of the fireworks and eventually I confronted the actual fireworks display. I now can watch a display but some of the loud sounds still disturb me. One thing I cannot desensitize myself to is the sound of the telephone ringing at night when I am asleep. I jump up and cannot stop the adrenaline from pumping. In Vietnam when the phone would ring we would be airborne and shooting within two minutes. I may never be able to desensitize myself to that one. The goal of the therapy should be to promote a sense of recovery and a feeling that you have mastered your anxiety. Studies of behavior therapy have shown that it is effective, and the prognosis for long-term success is excellent.

Medication

Tranquilizers decrease the feelings of anxiety. **Antidepressants** called (SSRIs) Selective Serotonin Reuptake Inhibitors act on the chemical serotonin, which is the neurotransmitter in the brain that helps brain cells. The neurons send and receive messages in the brain. The following medications help control depression and anxiety: SSRIs Prozac, Zoloft, Celexa, Luvox, Paxil, and Effexor XR.

Couples Therapy

First, it is important to realize that couples therapy, marriage counseling and marital therapy are all the same. These different names have been used to describe the same process, with the difference often based on which psychotherapy theory is favored by the psychologist using the term, or whether an insurance company requires a specific name for reimbursement.

Couples therapy is often seen as different from psychotherapy because a relationship is the focus of attention, instead of one individual diagnosed with a specific psychological problem. This difference only arises if you consider psychological problems to be similar to medical illnesses, and therefore confined to a "sick" individual who needs treatment. That medical model of psychological diagnosis and treatment is common, but is really inadequate to describe and resolve psychological problems. All psychological problems, and all psychological changes, involve both individual symptoms (behavior, emotions, conflicts, thought processes) and changes in interpersonal relationships.

Couples therapy focuses on the problems existing in the relationship between two people. But, these relationship problems always involve individual symptoms and problems, as well as the relationship conflicts. For example, if you are constantly arguing with your spouse, you will probably also be chronically anxious, angry or depressed (or all three). Or, if you have difficulty controlling your temper, you will have more arguments with your partner.

In couples therapy, the psychologist will help you and your partner identify the conflict issues within your relationship, and will help you decide what changes are needed, in the relationship and in the behavior of each partner, for both of you to feel satisfied with the relationship.

These changes may be different ways of interacting within the relationship, or they may be individual changes related to personal psychological problems. Couples therapy involves learning how to communicate more effectively, and how to listen more closely. Couples must learn how to avoid competing with each other, and need to identify common life goals and how to share responsibilities within their relationship. Sometimes the process is very similar to individual psychotherapy, sometimes it is more like mediation, and sometimes it is educational. The combination of these three components is what makes it effective.

The Propinquity Effect

The definition of propinquity is the tendency for people to form friendships or romantic relationships with those whom they encounter often. The key word is often. Relationships tend to be formed between those who have propinquity. At MIT in the early fifties, Leon Festinger, Stanley Schacter, and Kurt Back, psychologists, discovered the phenomenon. Propinquity is also explained by just being in the proximity of one another.

Synonyms for propinquity in the context of a noun relative to contact are touching, approximation, nearness, proximity, union, contingence, strike, closeness, contiguity, and relation.

Synonyms for propinquity in the context of a noun relating to proximity are nearness, togetherness, closeness, concurrence, and adjacency.

Synonyms for propinquity in the context of a noun relating to vicinity are area, vicinage, turf, territory, district, environment, surroundings, proximately, region, locality, and hood.

Synonyms for propinquity in the context of a noun as it relates to a neighborhood are community, closeness, ghetto, block, confines, jungle, slum, suburb, territory, turf, surroundings, parish, precinct, vicinity, and war zone.

Synonyms for propinquity in the context of a noun as it relates to relation are connection.

The main thrust of this discussion is to educate us in regard to the consequences of the deprivation of propinquity as it relates to relationships. What prompted this discussion is the absence of propinquity as a result of my business relations over the past number of years; and also, the discovery of the propensity toward the propinquity effect among the wives, children, and families who live with and are affected by PTSD.

Seventeen years ago I was downsized from the corporate world from a major corporation for the third time. I told my wife we were going to sell the house and start our own business – a Human Resource Management consulting firm called "Business Team Builders."

When I was in the Navy, the propinquity effect was incredibly wonderful and satisfying. A side benefit of this effect was knowing that someone was there and helping you, which makes your life less stressful. Even though pilots were in a sense competing against each other, the camaraderie between pilots and air crewmen was unbelievable. The effect was always at its maximum whether it was war or peace.

We would have weekly "All Pilots Meetings." We would sit in the squadron ready room with flight jackets on – patches and all, drink coffee and tell jokes. We would study Russian aircraft, submarines, and ships. On Friday afternoons we would all go to happy hour. We flew together, lived on the same ship together, and lived in the same neighborhoods. We had monthly squadron social events, sometimes with the children, so the children were very close also.

Lifelong friendships and relationships were forged. When we would go overseas, our shipmates would look out for each other's families. One incident that comes to mind concerns a pregnant wife whose husband was overseas. The wife called and said "The labor pains are close together, can you drive me to the hospital?" I jumped into the car and sped to the hospital. When we arrived, the nurse wanted her to fill out some forms for admission. I was as nervous as a cat and paced the floor, worrying that the baby would be born in the admissions office. They finally came back and brought her to a room and the nurse came out and told me I could go in and see my wife. I laughed and said, "Oh! She's not my wife." The nurse cracked up. There were hundreds of incidents like this that accentuated propinquity at its best at all levels.

The relationship between military, aircrew, and door gunner is one of the greatest examples of the propinquity effect. They bond with togetherness and closeness and are members of an immediate circle with association, kinship, and the connection that makes it work.

After my 22 years in the Navy I entered the corporate world … a whole other world. Working for the Restaurant, Airline, Ship Repair, Rehabilitation and Quick Lube industries, I worked tirelessly to build the propinquity effect. It was almost impossible and I had very little success. There is propinquity in the corporate world, but nowhere near the intensity as it is in the service, although I did make some lasting relationships and friendships. We did party on occasion, usually around the holidays. The relationships were not necessarily within department lines, but were frequently formed because of age or interests. Sometimes the relationships were formed because of previous military experiences. Military people bonded by deep common interests. Corporate people have some of the tenants, but the effect is barely recognizable.

After the last downsizing, we started our own business. We have been extremely fortunate throughout the 17 years of business, since we have been able to keep contracts for up to two years, which have been substantial. In fact, one government contract has lasted for the entire 17 years and is still going.

The problem when you become a business owner is that propinquity immediately drops almost to zero. Associations with someone you have a contract with is just that – an association. It doesn't even come close to equating with the propinquity effect.

Only in a few instances have I been able to form a lasting relationship with someone who I service on a contractual basis. There is very little in common to enable a relationship to surface in this environment.

A consultant is an outsider, and in many cases considered the enemy. The CEO and other executives will accept your ideas and suggestions for a solution, but that is as far as it goes. You may have lunch, or be invited to an occasional party, but you will never be accepted into the inner sanctum and have the propinquity effect be allowed to take place.

During the course of our business ventures, I have written and published a number of articles on various subjects. My wife has edited them and has made some very excellent enhancing suggestions. I finally realized that she should receive credit for her work so I said, "Let's put both our names as the authors." This was the beginning of the propinquity effect within our business and our marriage.

Even though we have become members of organizations, such as the American Psychological Association, the State Psychology Association, etc. there is some but very little propinquity within these groups. That is not to say that there is not bonding or closeness, but it is not the same. A few friendships may arise, but there generally is very little togetherness, or kinship among the groups.

In high-profile, high-pressure environments, the loss of propinquity can be psychologically debilitating. This is why executive burnout is a common occurrence. The lack of the effect in helping professions is particularly disturbing. Psychiatrists, psychologists, and physicians are especially vulnerable to this phenomenon, mainly because the competition is so intense and they tend to air any weaknesses or shortcomings.

In my research for this book. *The Man I Didn't Know*, I have been overwhelmed by the incredible amount of the presence of the propinquity effect. The wives and families of the veterans affected with PTSD all share the same common problems. They all face the same decisions, and the same behavioral problems exhibited by their veteran. They have formed associations, relationships, kinship, friendships, become close and have become affiliated with like groups all in the same situation. The support groups, the wives groups, the family groups and the therapeutic situations help to cement the propinquity effect.

What can we do to promote the propinquity effect? I strongly suggest that wives, families, and children become involved in support groups and form a relationship within a core group that shares the same common interests and problems.

Stress Management

We have chosen to deal with the subject of stress management as a separate issue because of the importance of the subject. It is extremely important that vets and the families learn how to manage stress, particularly during the times that the vet is exhibiting his or her PTSD behavior.

Exactly What is Stress?

It is what we experience in our daily lives that makes demands on our mind/body system. Notice I said mind/body system. This is to emphasize the part the mind plays on the body's stress response. Ninety-eight percent of the response is subjective and two percent is objective. Our perception of the stressor and our ability to cope is what affects our body in a very distinctive way, either good or bad.

If we stay on the stressed side (sympathetic side) of the nervous system for long periods of time, the biochemical reactions will affect every organ in our body in an adverse way. These reactions will in turn decrease the power of our immune system, and make us subject to illness and disease. Obviously, we need to learn how to halt the destruction and return to the stress-less side of the nervous system (parasympathetic).

"Stress is the spice of life. Complete freedom from stress is death," says Hans Selye, MD. Actually, stress becomes a matter of concern when there is too much of it, and too few coping skills to deal with it appropriately. Just as exercise can increase muscle strength, stress can make us stronger, if we deal with it in a positive manner.

Too much of anything is bad: too much water can kill you, too many vitamins can kill you, and too much relaxation can turn you to mush. But in the right amounts they are essential for life. A little stress can make life interesting. Too much can make you ill. So how do we learn coping skills so that our everyday stressors don't accumulate to the point of overwhelming us?

First of all, we need to acknowledge the stress. Sometimes all it takes to diffuse the small day-to-day stresses is to realize that they are there and then decide to do something about them. Next we need to prioritize the stresses. Put them in proper perspective so that they are based on reality rather than our overactive imagination. Then we need to examine the self-talk. Are things really as bad as they seem, or are we making a problem that does not exist? Then we will have the energy to deal with the reality.

There are many coping skills that have proven to be effective. Some of them are as follows:

Coping Skills

1. Breathe correctly. One of the most effective coping skills we can learn is to breathe correctly.

2. Time management. We live in a society that is on the go most of the time, which makes the effective use of our time a critical issue.

3. Communicate assertively. Ineffective communication creates a great deal of stress. Communicating assertively helps improve relationships and reduce stress.

4. Role expectation. Knowing what is expected in advance can prevent many misunderstandings.

5. Learning the importance of good nutrition during times of stress.

6. Relaxation skills such as creative visualization and meditation. Relaxing won't solve your problems, but it will make it easer for you to see how to solve them for yourself.

7. Exercise, which creates and releases opiate-like chemicals called endorphins and encephalins. Exercise produces natural painkillers, which help with depression and aid with weight loss.

8. And last, one of the strongest is humor. Laughter is said to be "healthy internal jogging." It has been shown to improve immune functioning and increase our ability to withstand pain. Even smiling, whether you mean it or not, has been shown in studies to reset the nervous system and create beneficial chemicals in the body.

It may be quite difficult for the vet to do some or all of these, but the families must practice some or all of these methods to cope with the stressful lifestyle. The bottom line is that we must work very diligently to live a balanced life, expose ourselves to new ways of handling difficult situations, and learn how to manage our stress effectively. Stress can be a killer. Happy, optimistic people live longer and are healthier. So smile while you are coping.

Stress Results

As stress increases, the energy available to the mind/body system decreases. As stress increases, perception decreases. As perception decreases, the ability to interpret incoming data decreases. Communications are defective and the accuracy diminishes. The stressor becomes more powerful and takes control. An increase in stress results in a decrease in perception, auditory, visual, tactile, and spatial. All forms of conceptual capacity decrease as stress levels continue to accelerate, or remain at high levels without interruption for extended periods of time. Accidents, illnesses, injuries, and poor communication follow naturally when stress levels remain high and effective interventions are not provided. We must learn new coping skills and we must learn to reframe the stressor, or, in other words, look at the stressor in a different light, a more favorable light. Reduce the subjective components and increase the objective components.

Objective and Subjective Components of Stress

Objective components:

1. Deadlines
2. Production quotas
3. Long work hours
4. Interruptions
5. Loud noises
6. Too many people around

Subjective components:

1. I am going to lose my job.
2. I am going to lose my house.
3. I am going to lose my car.
4. My wife is going to leave me.
5. We are going to have an earthquake.
6. Loud noises and fireworks startle me.
7. I am just stupid.
8. My kids hate me.
9. I am going to die.

The subjective components must be reframed and looked at in a different light. Using all of the stress management procedures will allow the vet and the families to cope with the prevailing stressors. The most effective procedure to manage stress is reframing the stressor.

Stress Reducing Procedures

To lower the level of stress that you experience:

1. Examine your perception of the stressor, it is probably in error.
2. Clearly identify your coping skills.
3. Examine your coping skills, they may be better than you think.
4. Examine negative coping skills.
5. Improve existing positive coping skills.
6. Improve or develop new coping skills.
7. Alter the stressor if possible.
8. Move away from the stressor if possible.
9. Create a new self definition and image.
10. Use relaxation technologies.
11. Develop and practice nutritional behavior.
12. Create new beliefs and values.
13. Eliminate destructive beliefs and values.

Responsibility, Reliability, Reality

The following theory for the treatment of PTSD was developed by me a number of years ago. I have used the techniques to cope with my anxiety and depression. It has served me well. However, as I get older and work on this book my flashbacks, nightmares, hyper-vigilance and anger is almost out of control and being responsible, reliable and living in reality is not cutting it. I know I must go into treatment to deal with old monsters grown up.

I am of the opinion that these techniques of Responsibility, Reliability and Reality can be very effective in the treatment of wives and children who are affected by Post Traumatic Stress Disorder.

The following is the genesis of a theory that I have been working on for a number of years. It is called "Responsibility Therapy," and may someday be used to treat Post Traumatic Stress Syndrome and related mental disorders that occur because of a traumatic event. This theory was developed after I finished my education in psychology, and that is when I realized the relationship between responsibility therapy and Post Traumatic Stress Syndrome.

Studies have shown that 81.5% of the population (Srole, et al., 1962) is somewhat emotionally disturbed, which means that 18.5 percent remaining take care of the bulk of humanity. Is it in the realm of possibility that some of the 81.5 percent could take responsibility for not being mentally ill? There is no doubt in my mind that this could be the case. In my opinion humanistic psychology is not built on reading, writing and arithmetic. The foundation is responsibility, which diagrammed hierarchically looks like this:

Responsibility

Reality   **Reliability**

Responsibility is what makes people function in reality and become reliable citizens of the earth. Webster, et al., defines responsibility as follows: (1) The state or fact of being responsible; (2) Instance of being responsible; (3) A particular burden or obligation upon a person who is responsible; (4) Something for which a person is responsible; (5) Reliability or dependability; (6) Answerability; (7) Accountability. Man's most intrinsic quality is *responsibility*, which is the core of this therapy. I strongly believe that some mental illness is a conscious decision to abdicate the position of responsibility. When a person has no sense of purpose, he follows the path of least resistance, becoming apathetic, neurotic and eventually psychotic. Immature or undisciplined people are dominated by emotion. There are some people who truly believe that if they don't do anything, they won't fail. They also feel, at the same time, or all of the time, that it is better to decide *not* to decide. For those people who choose to escape from responsibility and reality, there is always intoxication, drugs or suicide.

Every individual is responsible for his own behavior. The therapist should never take responsibility for the patient's behavior. If a person has abdicated their responsibility and chooses to be mentally ill, they must somehow be brought back to reality. They must take hold and nurture the responsibility of their actions back to a healthy position. There will never be any change in one's behavior unless they accept the fact that they alone are responsible for it. This should not be a struggle, as it is to some, to behave in a responsible manner. A person must be creative in his or her own environment, and they must be responsible for their reality in the sense that they can either let it come to a standstill or actively change it. External influences *do* affect the situation, but are *not* the ultimate determining factors.

The responsible position in life should be accepted, within the mentally healthy position and within the framework of reality. Once again, this should not be a struggle, as it is to some, to behave in a responsible manner. In order to function in reality, we must first learn how to act responsibly. I agree with Glasser that a responsible person does that which gives them a feeling of self-worth and a feeling that is worthwhile to others. I strongly believe that a person who doesn't get off of their backside loses it, which is theorized in the evolution discussion. I also agree with Glasser that "People do not act irresponsibly because they are ill; they are ill because they act irresponsibly." For example, the alcoholic or drug addict acts irresponsibly to deny reality and escape it. People who are mentally ill deny reality (Glasser, 1965). The underlying assumption to responsibility therapy is similar to Glasser's reality therapy in that we must direct the client toward more responsible behavior, which is reality oriented, so that a person can be a functioning, reliable person in society. The therapist must guide the client to make a commitment, a concrete decision to act responsibly and give up the ways of irresponsibility. Unlike psychiatry, we must not concern ourselves with the archives and the cobwebs of the past. It is not important how we got there, but it is extremely important to find out what we should do to stay here in reality, to be reliable, and to act responsibly.

What can we do to give our lives a responsible base so that we can become reliable citizens with a reality orientation? Well, we can first make the decision to act in a responsible manner. The book *One Flew Over the Cuckoo's Nest*, which was turned into a popular movie, is a classic example of a person making such a decision. It is an excellent portrayal of psychiatric patients making the decision to act irresponsibly and choosing the mentally ill position to cope with reality.

Some people fail at choosing to be mentally ill. Could it be that when they make the decision to be mentally ill, they fail so badly because of paradoxical intention? Freedom to choose and make a responsible decision together makes man a spiritual being. If the therapist wishes to foster his client's mental health, he should not be afraid to increase the burden of the client's responsibility to fulfill the meaning of his existence (Frankel, 1967). This should also be the case in raising children. As a child grows older, the child should gradually take responsibility for his or her behavior so that they are fully responsible at adulthood.

Shostrom believes the shift in responsibility for a child's life occurs around eleven or twelve. The responsibility level should be equal between the child and the parent. As the child becomes older, the responsibility shifts to them for their own behavior. In the case of the child, responsibility is difficult to learn for it is outside the younger child's control. Young children must have frequent reminders if they are to learn responsibility. In short, children have to gradually be taught responsibility from an early age (Shostrom, 1967).

The person who rejects awareness, spontaneity, and intimacy also rejects the responsibility for shaping his own life. To make a responsible decision, we must also consider the fact that this decision must be a realistic, attainable one (i.e., an alcoholic who makes the responsible decision to quit using alcohol cannot be successful if he is in the middle of a traumatic experience or exposing himself to a social environment with his drinking buddies every night after work). We must set ourselves up for a win/win situation and not a win/lose or a lose/lose situation. The alcoholic who is still drinking, and the person who has chosen to be mentally ill, are both setting themselves up for failure. The alcoholic must make a realistic commitment to quit drinking and take responsibility for his or her behavior. If that person takes responsibility for their behavior, they will be rewarded by an ever-increasing sense of strength, competence and security. Complete identification with oneself can only take place if a person is willing to take full responsibility for his or her actions, thoughts, and feelings, and by ceasing to confuse responsibility and obligation. Some people believe that responsibility means, "I put myself under obligation to you." Under no circumstances does it mean that. You are responsible for yourself and your behavior, and I am responsible for my behavior and myself. If a patient decides to act irresponsibly and commits suicide, then it is *their* responsibility, and not yours. If the individual chooses to be mentally ill, then it is *their* business until that behavior infringes on society in a harmful way. Responsibility is not a given way to behave, but an unavoidable must. We, as citizens of the earth, are the responsible doers of whatever we carry out. The only alternatives we have are either to acknowledge responsibility or totally deny it. I am not totally in agreement with the position existentialists take when they say, "We are not only responsible for ourselves, but we are responsible for what becomes of others." This school of thought believes in existential anguish, which is what a person feels in bearing the burden of responsibility for all mankind. It is the realization that, in making a responsible decision for themselves, they have chosen the position which is sought after by most of mankind (Kapin, 1961). A person is free and well when he accepts the responsibility of his choices. Therefore, if he is oriented to reality, he must choose whatever is in his own best interests.

The patient is the one who changes his attitude toward his fears or other problems, and therefore cures himself of them. This focuses the responsibility on the patient and prevents him from becoming dependent on the therapist. The patient must detach himself from the neurosis. The ultimate goal of responsibility therapy is that the patient should be able to learn to make responsible choices and decisions. Patients should grow in their awareness of their ability and responsibility to cope with a situation in a reality-oriented way. It is my opinion that there would not be 81.5% of the population who are mentally disturbed if we taught responsible behavior at an early age. What happens if this is done at an early age but the training is interrupted by a traumatic event like war? Then the responsibility training has to be accomplished again so the individual can learn that they should not abdicate their responsible position in life. Responsibility can be learned at any age, however it is easier to learn correct behavior initially than to overcome previous bad learning (Glasser, 1975). Glasser further states, and I agree with him, that responsibility should be learned early at home and in school rather than from a therapist. Responsibility fosters (i.e. perpetuates) mental health and irresponsibility fosters mental illness.

People in our society today do not realize the importance of responsibility and the role it plays in their lives. They think that it comes naturally and easily, and can be turned on and off. This perverse feeling about the nature of responsibility, I believe, is the genesis of mental illness. Persons who do not learn responsibility or do not accept it are the ones who, in prisons or mental institutions, are punished twice as much. Glasser says this, because that person had it in his power not to get drunk. Aristotle says, "Man is responsible to himself for being unjust or self-indulgent." This is true because he has the power not to be that way (Glove, 1970). Therapists sometimes consider it pointless to treat persons who have chosen to abdicate the responsibility of life. Who is morally responsible, the abdicator or the therapist? As I have said earlier, the therapist should not take responsibility for the actions of the patient. The therapist *does* have a moral obligation to serve the patient in the best way, but he *cannot* in this case.

Therapists and patients alike do not always teach responsibility. The therapist may tell their psychotic patient that they must keep their room clean, but if they don't do it, they shrug it off; if they do, they expect it. The parent acts in the same manner; therefore, in either case, responsible actions are not taught and reinforced. We do not set high enough expectations for ourselves, or others for that matter. We become lackadaisical in our daily lives, which encourages irresponsible behavior. F.H. Bradley states the position that there is a logical link between the ordinary man's concept of responsibility and the liability to punishment. He says that, for practical purposes, we need not make a distinction between responsibility or accountability, and liability to punishment. Where you have the other, and where you don't have one, you don't have the other (Glove, 1970).

I agree with Laing et al. that a good deal of schizophrenia and Post Traumatic Stress Syndrome is simply nonsense, prolonged filibustering to throw dangerous people off the scent, and to create boredom and futility in others. The mentally ill patient is often making a fool of himself, and the therapist. The patient is playing at being insane to avoid, at all costs, the possibility of being held responsible and accountable for a single coherent idea or intention (Laing, 1965). Jung confirms this by the statement that the schizophrenic ceases to be schizophrenic when he meets someone whom he feels understands him. When this happens, most of the bizarre behaviors, which were taken as signs of the disease, simply disappear (Laing, 1965). We expect people to act crazy in a mental ward and they do conform to that behavior. Laing argues that the behavior of schizophrenics is generally an intelligible response to the world as they see it, and that their actions are at least as rational as the actions of more normal people (Laing, 1965). In addition, Laing argues that schizophrenic behavior is a natural response to certain types of human situations, which have resulted from contradictory demands made upon people by their relationships with others, especially members of their families. He describes the schizophrenic experience as a "voyage into inner space and time." He says that we no longer can assume that such a voyage is an illness that has to be treated. This is just another way to abdicate responsibility and escape from the reality of this so-called normal world. American society today uses all sorts of ways to escape. Our society is a drug-oriented society. Just watch television and see what the commercials tell us, not to mention MTV and shows like Survivor. We use alcohol or drugs or whatever it takes to take our voyages. Seems to me, if we learned responsible behavior, we would not want to escape. There are so many things that have to be accomplished in such a short time.

If we keep a reality-oriented base for our lives, we could deal with the trauma which comes with daily living. We would not have to live a life filled with irresponsibility. We beat ourselves down when the first failure comes along, then we look at what a failure we are and choose to make ourselves depressed and anxious. In order to live a full and happy life, we must not feed our neuroses. We must stand up to these feelings of inadequacy that we harbor within ourselves, and use them to perpetrate the hoax that we are not mentally healthy.

We must choose to be mentally well; we must take the course of responsible action in order to complete the difficult task of living in a chaotic world where most people choose the path of irresponsibility. If we cannot do it ourselves, we must ask for help. First, we have to recognize the fact that we need help. This is the difficult part, but it can be identified with just a fraction of attention to our lives. I realize that even when we set out with this goal in mind, the process may be interrupted by inattention, poor communication, a traumatic experience, divorce or even another war with no name. This is when, as soon as possible, an outsider should intervene; another adult or a therapist should take over the process of teaching responsibility. If there is not an intervention for some time, the situation will deteriorate as the person takes on the irresponsible position. They choose to no longer cope and they abdicate their responsibility with escapes from reality. As Tillich writes, "Neurosis is the way of avoiding non-being by avoiding being," or in my words, not taking responsibility for our behavior. The process may be slow or rapid, but can be interrupted at any time. In the early stages of neurosis, a person sets himself up for failure. He consistently tells himself, either consciously or subconsciously, that he is depressed and anxious. The recovering alcoholic who has been sober for some time knows that all they have to do is take the first drink and they are off on the path to destruction. Sometimes they reward themselves for being so good and living a model life. In any case, they set themselves up for failure by choosing the path of least resistance and irresponsible behavior. People who commit suicide have set themself up for ultimate failure, as evidenced by the fact that they tell no less than ten persons before they do it.

Once a sound, responsible base is established, growth can occur in one's life. Hierarchically, the next step is reality orientation, which leads to continued mental health and builds a reliable person. I believe that there are three main thrusts to responsibility therapy: reality, responsibility, and reliability. In order to be responsible you must live in reality and be reliable. In order to be reliable, you must choose to act responsibly and live in reality. In order to live in reality, you must act responsibly and be reliable. If we choose not to be responsible, we cannot live in reality and we cannot be reliable or be counted on to be a responsible citizen of the world.

It is my opinion that a number of Vietnam veterans have abdicated their responsibility and have chosen to opt out of life. They refuse to take responsibility for their actions. They escape by becoming dependent on drugs or alcohol. Some have become street people and some have chosen to be mentally ill. When we were young and thought we were invincible we chose an irresponsible position in life. In order to cope with stresses of the War, we drank alcohol on our days off and we did speed on the days we flew. Most of us recovered from our irresponsible behavior. We managed not to do any damage to either ourselves or anyone else and were able to fight and maintain a reasonable daily position in a hellhole. Most of us have come to live useful and productive lives. Some didn't recover and chose to live in another reality, to become unreliable citizens, and to not take responsibility for their lives. What we must do to treat a Post Traumatic Stress Syndrome patient who is not malingering is to show them the reality of the existence that they have chosen. We must help them choose a responsible position in reality and become a reliable person. How do we do that? It's a question of retraining the individual to learn responsibility again in their lives. We must deprogram the sights and sounds that were acquired from participating in the war by either desensitizing or exposure therapy. The individual must force himself to go to fireworks at a Fourth of July celebration, desensitizing the mind to the loud noises and bright lights. We must transform the celebration of the 4th of July into a celebration and not a firefight in the jungle in the middle of the night. As the world becomes smaller and there are more Vietnamese immigrants into the United States we must learn to assimilate our thoughts to the present day and not think of our involvement with these people years ago. We must teach the Post Traumatic Stress Syndrome patient to learn to accept the here and now and how the world is, in its present state, and *not* how it was thirty years ago in the jungle.

As I see life's continuum from our historical perspective, we make a decision to be a lost soul or a responsible person in our society as follows: We all come with our historical perspective – where did we come from, how did we live, and when were we put in a particular time and place? We live through the circumstances of life. We then make decisions whether to go to college or go to the military or become a draft dodger. We sometimes have no control over these decisions and we are asked to join the military.

The results of these decisions change the course of our lives. If we found ourselves in a "War With No Name," then we must deal with how this trauma affected us. We can choose specific actions and behaviors, ignore the trauma or let it affect our lives. The consequences of our actions could be alcohol, drug abuse, or mental illness.

We must make a decision at this point to either abdicate and become mentally ill or act responsibly. The therapist must reintroduce the concept of taking responsibility back into the life of the Post Traumatic Stress Syndrome patient. When they choose not to abdicate they then can live in reality and become productive reliable citizens. These concepts are interwoven and perpetuate mental health. What I have tried to do in this chapter is bring together some salient ideas of my own and others concerning the concept of responsibility and how it relates to Post Traumatic Stress Syndrome.

I would hope that these ideas will open some doors and foster some thought concerning another way of looking at mental health and well-being as it relates to the veteran and Post Traumatic Stress Syndrome.

Art Schmitt, Ph.D.

Where Do We Get Such Men?

Every time a therapist asks a veteran, his husband or wife, "When were they last in combat?" The answer is always the same, "Last night." That statement really sums up the story of the Vietnam veteran and any war veteran. This has been the story of their struggle to live with PTSD.

The symptoms described in every person's story are almost always the same but affect the individuals in varying degrees.

The families cope with the results of the disorder in many different forms. These coping skills include anything from suicide to divorce. This book will attempt to teach the families good coping skills so that they don't have to turn to such drastic measures. The main objective of the book is to show the families they are not alone in this struggle and to help them live with PTSD.

As we have discussed, the wives and families must live their own lives, have friends and pursue outside interests. They must be responsible for their actions, be reliable and live in reality. They must learn how to convert the grieving process to the serenity process.

Symptoms that are identified most frequently occurring among veterans are: isolation, agoraphobia, survivor's guilt, anger and rage, depression, sleep disturbances, flashbacks, and nightmares. In addition, sometimes suicide ideation is present and persistent, and occasionally suicide takes place.

The families have to recognize these symptoms and know the emotions of the vet and identify that they are real and they have to be dealt with on a day-to-day basis. The main theme that echos throughout the stories is that initially when the families are confronted with the veteran's PTSD, they don't understand or comprehend the consequences or the magnitude of the disorder. Along with the veteran, the families sometimes stay in denial forever and never go for treatment. Wives and children must take every opportunity to learn about PTSD. They need to read books concerning the subject. Suggested readings will appear in the appendix.

We strongly urge family members to seek therapy and become involved in support groups. Group therapy is extremely helpful in the healing process because the families are made aware of similar problems. Families are able to commiserate and discuss how they have handled similar family situations. Relationships are formed and friendships are made within the framework of the group, which are therapeutic. This also applies to couples, group, marriage, and family therapy. It is recommended that couples enter into a therapeutic relationship if the PTSD is interfering with the normal functioning of day-to-day life. The main advantage of these therapies is that the participants can give and receive feedback, encouragement, support, or criticism. The other advantage is that participants will realize that they are not alone and may share the same problems and feelings. The therapy focuses on interpersonal interactions, so relationship problems are addressed well in groups.

Therapy involves learning how to communicate more effectively, and how to listen more closely. The goal should be to learn how not to compete with each other, identify common life goals, and share responsibilities within the relationship. This process is extremely difficult to achieve considering the symptoms of people affected by PTSD and is not always achievable.

In closing I would like to reflect on the appropriate words of James Michener, 1983, as they were spoken by the Admiral on the bridge of an aircraft carrier as he observed the flight operations in the movie *Bridges at Toko Ri*.

"Why is America lucky enough to have such men?

They leave this tiny ship and fly against the enemy.

Then they must seek the ship lost on the sea and

when they find it, they have to land upon its pitching deck."

"Where do we get such men?"

That was a movie about the Korean War but the sentiment is there for the courageous service people who serve in all wars. Where did we get such men and women who served so gallantly, who took so much abuse and came out with lasting scars within them and their families?

Books Worth Reading

A War With No Name . . . . Dr. Art Schmitt

Recovering from the War . . . . Patience Mason

Vietnam Wives . . . . Aphrodite Matsakis

Lonely Girls With Burning Eyes . . . . Marian Novak

Achilles in Vietnam . . . . Jonathan Shay, MD., Ph.D.

A Knight in Rusty Armor . . . . Robert Fisher

On the Tiger's Back . . . . Bernard E. Grady

The Power of Positive Thinking . . . . Norman Vincent Peale

Feeling Good . . . . David D. Burns

I Touch the Earth the Earth Touches Me . . . . Hugh Prather

Meditations From the Road Less Traveled . . . . M. Scott Peck, MD

The Tao of Pooh . . . . Benjamin Hoff

The Te of Piglet . . . . Benjamin Hoff

The New Three Minute Meditator . . . . David Harp

101 Simple Ways to Be Good to Yourself . . . . Donna Watson, Ph.D.

Any Book by John Bradshaw

Any Book by Melody Beattie

If you have a computer, type in Post Traumatic Stress Disorder for more information.

For an informative website: *vetsoutreach.com*

Click on: *WIFELINE* to find a newsletter written "for women who live with veterans".

If you have any questions about *The Man I Didn't Know,* or if you would like an autographed copy please email:

Dr. Art Schmitt . . . . docbtb@bellsouth.net

Marie Leduc . . . . rosesforvets@yahoo.com

References Cited

Adams, J.D., *Understanding and Managing Stress*, San Diego, CA, University Associates, Inc. 1980.

Borysenko, J., Ph.D., with Rothstein, L., *Minding the Body, Mending the Mind*, New York, Bantam Books, 1985.

Cooper, G.L., Payne, R., *Stress at Work*, New York, John Wiley & Sons.

Girdano, D.E., Ph.D., Everly, G.S., Ph.D., Dusek, D.E., Ph.D., *Controlling Stress and Tension, A Holistic Approach*, Fourth Edition, Englewood Cliffs, New Jersey, Prentice Hall, 1993.

Goldberger, L., Breznitz, S., *Handbook of Stress*, Second Edition, New York, The Fress Press, A Divison of Macmillan, Inc., 1982.

Hanson, P.G., M.D., *The Joy of Stress*, New York, Andrews and McMell, 1985.

Harkness, Laurie, Ph.D., *The Effect of Combat-Related PTSD on Children*, National Center for Post Traumatic Stress Disorder, 1991.

Hoffman, E., M.D., *Our Health Our Lives*, New York, Pocket Books, 1998.

Kirsta, A., *The Book of Stress Survival*, New York, Simon and Schuster, 1986.

Kutash, I.L., Schlesinger, L.B. and Associates, *Handbook on Stress and Anxiety*, San Francisco, Jossey-Bass Publishers, 1980.

Other References

A War With No Name: Post Traumatic Stress Syndrome: A Survivors Story, Dr. Art Schmitt, CDR USN Retired, 2004.

Boots, Echoes of Vietnam, Pete Freas, 2003.

Seawolf 28, Al Billings, 2004.

Recovering from the War, A Woman's Guide to Helping Your Vet, Your Family and Yourself, Patience, H.C. Mason, Viking Press, 1990.

Sticker Shock Over Shell Shock, Behind the Walls of Ward 54, Mark Benjamin, Salon.com.

Vietnam Wives, Women and Children Surviving Post Traumatic Stress Disorder, Aphrodite Matsakis, Ph.D.

Author Information

Art Schmitt, PhD

Retired as a Commander, USN after 22 years serving as a Naval Aviator in various Command and Staff positions throughout the world. He worked in the corporate world as the Vice President of Human Resources in major corporations including two restaurant chains, A Pain Center, a quick lube company and an International airline. For the past 17 years he has been the owner of a Human Resource Management Consulting Company, Business Team Builders.

Presently he is serving as an expert witness for the Office of Hearings and Appeals, Social Security Administration as an independent contractor. He has a PhD in Psychology and is licensed in five states. During his three tours in Vietnam he was awarded a Distinguished Flying Cross, Bronze Star, 21 Air Medals and a Vietnamese Air Medal.

Recently he published a book concerning his three tours in Vietnam called, *A War With No Name* Post Traumatic Stress Disorder, a survivor's story. He and his wife Marilyn reside in Charleston, SC.

Marie Leduc

Marie Leduc was born in Gardner, Massachusetts. At a young age her family moved to Southington, Connecticut where she spent most of her life.

She is a life member of Associates of Vietnam Veterans of America, the Disabled American Veterans Auxiliary and the Ladies Auxiliary VFW Post 10222 in Murphy, North Carolina.

Since 1985 she and her husband have been active in the awareness of the POW-MIA issue. They have actively taken part in the many vigils held throughout Connecticut and Massachusetts. She has also hosted two eight-hour and many one-hour vigils in Southington, Connecticut … in honor of her uncle who is MIA (BNR) from WWII. She was also chairperson of two vigils for Veterans of the Vietnam War in Middletown, Connecticut.

When her husband started counseling at the Vet Center in Hartford, Connecticut, she became aware of Post Traumatic Stress Disorder (PTSD). She has talked with many veterans, especially at the vigils, went for counseling herself at the Vet Center to learn more about PTSD, and had a wives group in her home for about a year. Because of this counseling and talking with the veterans, their wives and families, she started "WIFE LINE" a newsletter for wives and families who live with veterans. By doing this she hoped to help others understand PTSD and the affects it has on loved ones of veterans. You can read parts of "WIFE LINE" issues on the following web site. (vetsoutreach.com … click on "WIFE LINE")

It took her 27 years to realize how much the Vietnam War had affected her. That's when she wrote her story *Let's Come Home Together* about her first husband's tour in Vietnam, (they were married during his tour) and years later while married to her present husband she learned about PTSD. She told this story about how loved ones are also affected by war to many Vet Centers, VA's, veteran organizations and two cable TV stations.

She and her husband were full time RV'ers for about nine years, traveling throughout 49 states. She still loves to travel, and is willing to tell her story to any veterans organization.

Marie is the mother of two sons, Thom and Geoff Miller. She is a homemaker, who enjoys crafts and gardening. She and her husband George reside in Hayesville, North Carolina.